Painting rainbows with broken crayons

D0168253

Merry Christmas
Thanks for
all you do!
Kathy
1996

Painting rainbows with broken crayons

101 Prayers for Teachers, Parents and Other Caretakers

Bernadette McCarver Snyder

AVE MARIA PRESS
NOTRE DAME, INDIANA 46556

© 1995 by Ave Maria Press, Inc., Notre Dame, IN 46556

International Standard Book Number: 0-87793-547-5

Library of Congress Catalog Card Number: 94-79361

Cover and text design by Katherine Robinson Coleman

Cover and text illustration by Greg Langel

Printed and bound in the United States of America.

~Dedication~

I slept and I dreamt that life was all joy.
I awoke and saw that life was but service.
I served and understood that service was joy.
~R. Tagore~

This book is for the many teachers who have touched and guided my life. I dedicate it to my first teacher, my mother, and to a much later teacher, my son. I dedicate it to all who spend time with children—teachers, parents, pastors, counselors, youth ministers—those people who understand that such "service" can be joy.

~Introduction~

A pain in the neck, a lump in the throat—that's a child! Anyone who has ever lived with one, worked with one, "dealt" with one knows what a challenging but wonderful experience a child can be. This book is like a child's first **primer**—a basic resource to help you get started. Pronounced differently, a **primer** is something to help you set things in motion as one would do when priming a water pump or pouring gasoline into a carburetor.

However you pronounce it, this book can be your either/or. Like a primer, it's easy reading. Like a primer, it can help when you get stuck or stalled and need to get your motor going again.

It takes a look and a laugh at typical situations faced by those crisis-control experts—teachers, parents, counselors, or anyone who deals with the younger generation. And then it offers up a prayer for HELP!

If you've ever had one of those days when you needed a primer or a primer, this book was written for you.

~1~ You did *what*?

Look at me! Look at me!

See what I *DID*. See what I *FOUND*. See what I *MADE*. See what I *INVENTED*. See what I *BROKE*.

No, no—kids never call your attention to something they broke! But they DO want you to notice, to look at their every achievement and discovery. Well, I guess adults like that kind of attention too, Lord.

So remind us how important it is to stop, look, and listen to those young voices. Help us exult and rejoice with them as they discover things we have already seen or already know. Help us to give them our undivided attention—as we often wish for others to give to us.

And thank you, Lord, for the opportunity to look at the world again through the fresh, shiny, innocent eyes of youth. Forgive us if we ever think we are too busy to pass up such a generous gift, such a wondrous chance to start over and to really see all the things we missed the first time around.

It's often said that children are today's investment and tomorrow's dividend. Help us to invest wisely, Lord— not selfishly, not begrudgingly, but generously and joyously.

It's also said that teachers are people who make the little things in life count! Once we've taught those sweet little things to count numbers, Lord, help us to also teach them to recognize the things in life that really count!

Then we can shout to you and say,

Look, Lord, Look!

Look what I did.

Look what I accomplished.

Look what I taught!

~2~ Good things really do come in small packages

Out of the mouths of children come the strangest ideas. And I just love it, Lord!

One little boy's family "inherited" an aunt's dog—and he told everyone they got a "used" dog.

A little girl asked how many angels it took to make an angel food cake. Another kid said an epistle is the wife of an apostle!

And then, did you hear, Lord, how a little boy outlined YOUR job description? He said,

> One of God's jobs is making people. God never makes grownups, only babies. That's because babies are smaller and easier to make. And also because he won't have to waste his valuable time showing them how to walk and talk and think. God gives THAT job to parents and teachers.

The same little boy noted, "God hears everything so there must be a lot of noise going on in his head unless he has figured out some way to turn it off."

Well, Lord, I hope you haven't turned ME off today because I have a few more things for you to hear. I want you to hear how happy I am that you allow me to spend time with those children you made. You DID make them small so we would have to do all the processing and programming, but I'm grateful for that opportunity Lord. I'm happy you let us share in the finishing of your most important product.

And besides, it's so much fun to wonder what they're going to say next!

~3~ All creatures loud and small

How can something so small make so much noise, Lord? Every time I go to a movie I am introduced to the latest technological advancement in sound systems, but none of them can match the sound system YOU put into each small child. Kids can still make a fire engine siren sound like a lullaby.

Well, I guess you had your reasons, Lord. I guess grown-up ears must seem like a long way up to a small person trying to get attention. I guess the loudness makes up for the shortness.

But, Lord, these grown-up ears match my pencil today— they are both worn down to the nub. Could you please help me to turn down those remarkable sound systems? Just for a little while? Just one notch?

There must be a way to find their "pause" button. Maybe I could tell them they are in a hospital zone and the hospital police will put adhesive tape on their mouths if they don't keep quiet? No, I guess not. Maybe I could pass out gumdrops so their teeth will get glued shut? No, the silliness of the exercise would cause even more commotion.

I know what I'll do, Lord. I'll whisper. Maybe they'll think they're missing something and turn down their volume so they can hear what I'm saying. I WANT them to hear me because I have stories to tell and lessons to teach—your lessons, Lord.

I do thank you for entrusting me with these creatures loud and small. Now, Lord, help me to turn them—temporarily at least—into creatures quiet and learning.

~4~ You scratch my back and maybe I'll scratch yours

Lord, I loved that old story about the TV announcer who was interviewing a little boy and asked, "What kind of work does your father do?" The little boy replied, "He's a school principal and he knows everything." The announcer said, "Well, if he knows everything, what advice did he give you about being on TV?" The little boy answered, "He told me not to scratch, no matter where it itches."

That's advice I need to remember today, Lord. I have lots of itches. I'm so mad I'm itching for a fight. I want to scratch several people off my list. And I want to scratch this whole horse race that has me on the run.

Of course, I realize I am an adult—a mature person who must not act that way. Instead, I have to smile and scratch somebody's back, hoping mine will get scratched in return.

But, Lord, I am itching to say, "I quit. No more. That's it. I'm finished. Take care of your own dirty work from now on." And I've got itchy feet that are tempting me to hit the road and hitchhike to another galaxy.

I need sympathy, Lord. I need empathy. I need to get a grip on myself! How can I set a good example for the children I've told to be peacemakers when I'm the one who's itching for a fight? You're my only hope, Lord. Help me make peace with myself, pick up the pieces, and start all over—from scratch!

~5~ How networking is like Grandma's lace tablecloth

You remember Grandma's table, Lord? It always had that awful-looking lace tablecloth on it. I didn't like that cloth. It looked like a lot of matted string to me. But to Grandma, it was a vision of beauty.

I couldn't wait until Grandma would snatch off that "beautiful" cloth and cover the table instead with some of her "made with love" southern food. Everyone remembers how she fixed fried pork chops with gravy to go with the hot biscuits, fried eggs and homemade jelly for breakfast. What a way to start a day!

Strangely enough, what I remember most is her homemade pimiento cheese. She ALWAYS had a pot of that mixed up and ready to put on the table. Maybe she liked mixed up things. Maybe that's why she liked that lace tablecloth.

I was thinking about that today when I was invited to a networking session. That's one of the "in" things today, Lord— networking. We used to call it, "you wash my hand and I'll wash yours" but today they call it networking.

It really is wonderful, Lord. It gives us poor, tired childhood "experts" a chance to pick each other's brains. You know how it is, Lord—sometimes two people have the same problem and the first one thinks of the perfect solution while the second one racks the old brain for days and can't come up with one original thought. The next time they have similar problems, the tables turn and the second one thinks of a solution while the first one stews and sizzles. Networking can soothe the sizzle.

Thank you, Lord, for this new/old idea of networking. It reminds me of a smorgasbord. Everybody can bring a favorite idea and throw it on the table. And then all can feast together.

It's the perfect teacher's aide! It's the perfect parent's helper. But I've been rattling on, Lord, when all I wanted to do was ask you to help me to be generous.

Help me to eagerly share my bright ideas with others instead of hoarding them to myself so that I can take all the credit.

I do love credit, Lord. That's why I have all those charge cards. But that's another story. So back to the networking, Lord. Help me to share like my grandma did. Help me to remember how all those strings tied together made that tablecloth she loved—while one string alone would have just been one piece of string.

Remind me of that on those slow days, Lord, when I lag and drag like a piece of string. Help me to eagerly hold out my ideas to others while I latch on to theirs. Help us ALL as we work together to turn our strings into a comforting safety net.

Say! Maybe this networking will be a way to help me finally tie up some of those loose threads in my life! Thanks, Lord, I needed that.

~6~ Why does time drag when you're watching—but fly when you're not!

Sixty minutes make an hour but it only takes ONE minute to make a difference! Why is it, Lord, that when I turn my back for just a minute, THAT'S the minute when the beans get spilled, the pot boils over, or a secret is whispered that I needed to hear?

I sometimes feel like a spotter in a forest lookout tower. I look and look, watch and watch. I am alert, dutiful, and conscientious. But the minute I look away, a forest fire breaks out and soon turns into an inferno.

Lord, my mother told me she had eyes in the back of her head and I almost believed her. Now I wonder why you don't make ALL mothers and fathers and teachers with such eyes. It would solve a lot of our little problems—those "little" problems children can create for themselves and others in just an instant.

Teach me, Lord, to look at the right moment, listen at the right time, and be as observant as if my eyes could see in all directions at once. Teach me to spot a spill on the way, a boiling point approaching, or a cutting remark about to be whispered.

But if I can't learn THAT lesson, Lord, then teach me how to mop up the spills, turn down the heat, and hear YOUR whispers of reassurance above my silent screams.

~7~ If God had meant me to take field trips, why didn't he let me be a well-paid outfielder?

Well, here I am again, Lord, bouncing along on this big yellow bus. My vertebrae are vibrating, my ribs are rattling, my ears are exploding—and my stomach is sending SOS signals.

Yes, we're heading out on another fabulous field trip. Where will it be this time—a pumpkin patch, a dog museum, a riverboat, a science exhibit? Or maybe a used car lot? That's where we SHOULD be going so we could trade in this bus for something better, something more rideable, more modern. Like maybe a covered wagon!

Yes, Lord, I know that field trips are good for children but what about adults? Baseball players get paid big bucks for playing in an outfield but teachers and parents do NOT get equal pay for playing out in a field.

I admit that sometimes I do enjoy these field trips. In fact, I suspect I enjoy them more than the kids do. While I'm drinking in information from the exhibits, they're lining up at the drinking fountains. While I'm being educated, they're trying to jump off the riverboat, squash the biggest pumpkin, knock over something in the science exhibit, or get lost looking for the museum restroom. Actually, I guess they're not trying to do those things. They do them WITHOUT trying!

Lord, help me to look calm while I'm shouting "LOOK OUT!" Help me to smile while I wipe off the mud, ketchup, and unknown foreign substances from little fingers. Give me the gifts of patience and awareness so I can laugh at and even savor these endurance contests. That way we can ALL have a field day on field trips!

~8~ I want it down in black and white

Everything else is written down in black and white—laws, contracts, famous quotes, speeding tickets. So what about you, Lord—when are you going to put down in black and white exactly what you want? When are you going to give us a black-and-white contract, outlining what is right and wrong, good or bad? When are you going to tell us exactly how to live and how to teach?

Yes, I know you gave us the Ten Commandments and the Bible and some saintly people to inspire us and a few thunderbolts to get our attention. But I want some instructions in black and white.

On the other hand I would hate it if your WORLD was just black and white—no pinks or yellows, no aqua or avocado, no sky blue or sea green. You sure knew what you were doing when you splashed in all those brighteners. So I guess you knew what you were doing when you gave us that colorful thing known as free will.

I guess life is much more exciting when we have the opportunity every day to choose, select, elect, and opinionate. So thank you for that, Lord—but please help me to teach the children the difference between the primrose path and the yellow brick road. And when it comes to something really basic, help me to erase all the grays and teach your plain old black-and-white truth.

~9~ Is money the root of all education today?

I heard that it costs more today to AMUSE a child than it did to educate his or her father! And I'm not surprised. Maybe that's why amusement gets bigger bucks and bigger respect than education.

Unfortunately, the children of today are "amused" from the moment they are born. The typical tot of yesteryear would have been lucky to go through childhood with one rattle, one pull-toy, one pair of hand-me-down roller skates, and one bike picked up at a garage sale. Today's typical child starts out with a room full of gadgets and continues to amass more and more through the years until the kid's collection includes such high-ticket items as a personal TV, a personal phone, and a personal computer. How can even the most talented teacher attempting to instill the value of education compete with such high-tech amusement?

Lord, forgive us if we sometimes attempt to compete by playing the same game; by being more amusing than instructive, more contemporary than constructive, more concerned about being liked than being listened to and learned from. Remind us, Lord, that youth comes only once and some of our lessons can be taught only then. After that, a pattern of life is set and that's next to impossible to reshape.

Remind me that it's good to be a child's friend but first and foremost, I am the adult, the teacher, the role model, the one in charge, the leader. Help me to always lead in the right direction—YOUR direction. And you and I know, Lord, that your direction is often VERY amusing!

~10~ If these kids are so dumb, why do they keep outsmarting me?

You know, Lord, it would be silly for a doctor to treat only healthy people, a carpet cleaner to clean only new carpets, a charity to give only to rich people—so why do I complain about these kids being dumb? If they already knew everything, they wouldn't need me to teach them!

And yet, Lord, you and I both know that sometimes they seem to know more about some things than I do. And sometimes it doesn't take an awful lot of effort on their part to outsmart me!

O.K., so maybe I'm more gullible or trusting or naive than they are. Maybe I'm not as smart as I think I am. But certainly neither are they. They are still children and they NEED me in order to learn the things I have to teach, to listen to the things I have to say, to benefit from the books I have read and the experiences I have had and the love I can give them.

Help me to stay one step ahead of them, Lord. Some days it is so hard to outwit their efforts to avoid knowledge, but I MUST. It is my ministry and my privilege. Be with me, Lord, as I do my best to teach these oh-so-smart, yet oh-so-needy children.

~11~ How throwing stones in a glass house can raise your insurance premiums and your blood pressure

She's too structured. He's too undisciplined. She spends too much time on silly little details. He's got too many stick-in-the-mud ideas. She's always late. He never listens when you're trying to make a point.

What's wrong with these kids AND adults, Lord? Why are they so hard to work with? Why can't they get their act together? Why can't they do things the RIGHT way for once!

It's sure easy to throw stones, Lord—but I guess you can break a lot of glass and crack a lot of friendships that way. Maybe I better try throwing something softer—like maybe a few compliments, an occasional smile, a friendly pat on the back, or something more meaningful than "have a nice day."

That's something else I hate, Lord—those stupid words and phrases like *meaningful* and *have a nice day*. See, there I go again!

O.K., Lord, O.K. I don't like my own glass house getting shattered so I better start respecting the fragile houses others live in. Help me, Lord, to lower my blood pressure by adjusting my perceptions. Help me to look more closely, to look through and under and inside instead of just seeing the surface. Help me to see the OTHER SIDE instead of just MY side.

But, Lord, you can see ALL sides. Surely you have noticed that some of these people I work with are just impossible. Can't you do something with THEM while you're working on me?

~12~ Getting all tied up in a memory

Today I saw a little girl in church with a big bow in her hair, and I remembered when I was a little girl. On Sundays my mother and I would always wear our best dresses and I would carefully buckle my patent leather shoes. But, we were never ready to leave until my mother tied a huge fat bow on the top of my head. It probably looked ridiculous, but I felt so special, so dressed up. Then I would take hold of my daddy's hand and feel so proud, so safe, to be walking with him on the way to church.

Lord, I probably thought more about that hairbow than about you then. But maybe that was O.K. because today, whenever I see a little girl with a big hairbow, I think of you. I feel so safe knowing that I can walk with you today. Thank you, Lord.

How sad, Lord, that many children today have never held a father's hand—or worn a mother's handmade hairbow. Too many have never felt so special, so safe. Forgive us, Lord, for allowing that to be a fact of life in our world.

Help me, Lord, help us all, to hold YOUR hand and reach out the other hand to the children. Help us to show them that they ARE special and no matter how alone or lonely they are, they can reach out to YOU and you will walk with them.

Thank you, Lord, for my happy memories—and help me to make the kind of memories that today's children can cherish tomorrow.

~13~ The big yell theory

I've been doing it again, Lord—thinking that if I yell loudly enough, the children will hear what I'm saying. I KNOW there's nothing wrong with their hearing. I could get a bullhorn and shout it out but it wouldn't help them to pay attention. So why do I keep doing this, Lord? Why do I yell when I KNOW it will do no good—and might do some bad!

That's no way to teach—with volume. I don't want them to learn loudness. They already have enough of that—loud music, loud videos, loud world. I should be teaching calmness, gentleness, couth.

Well, that's not easy, Lord. It's not easy to remain calm in the midst of a monsoon. I was once told that I should be like the ocean. Though the ocean is buffeted by winds, churned with mile-high waves, and caught in storms of lightning and thunder, way way down in its depths the sea water remains calm, serene, unruffled. Well, I've been working to be like that, Lord. I know I must pray and meditate more if I am to attain more inner peace and deeper serenity. But so far, I'm still splashing.

Forgive me, Lord. I can't teach children to trust you in all things when I keep thundering out complaints, yelling instead of quelling! Calm me, Lord, so I can calm others.

And, Lord, forgive me if I've been yelling at YOU too—but you know, sometimes it seems as if YOU'RE as hard to reach as those children!

~14~ You've got a lotta nerve, he's got a lotta nerve, she's got a lotta nerve. No wonder we're all so nervous!

"I have one nerve left—and you're getting on it." When I saw those words on a T-shirt today, Lord, I knew it was my special message for the day.

Why is it that everybody today thinks it's admirable to have lots of nerve! I've had to have a lotta nerve to accomplish a lot of the things I've done in the past, I'll admit, but now my nerve is running low. And just when being nervy has come into style!

Today's children have the nerve to talk back to teachers and parents! We never did that. Today's kids have the nerve to skip class, skip homework, skip school—and then expect to skip through life! We might have wanted to do that but we knew better. Today's teens have the nerve to watch R-rated movies and TV shows and think it makes them mature enough to go out and try to live the same lifestyle. We weren't too smart but we were smarter than that.

Yes, Lord, today's children, from first grade to last, have got a lotta nerve. And it's getting on my nerve!

Help me, Lord, to show them that it takes MORE than nerve to have a happy, productive life. Help me to show them that it does sometimes take a lot of nerve AND determination AND work to succeed but that's very different from just being nervy!

Help the children AND me to learn the lesson that being nervy can get on somebody else's last nerve!

~15~ Why do they always have more questions than I have answers?

Guess what, Lord? I just learned today that in a seed plant, the *anther* is the part of the stamen that develops and contains pollen. Now at least I have one anther for the millions of questions the kids come up with every week!

Where do they find all those questions, Lord? And why can't I come up with answers? Once upon a time you could sagely tell a child to look it up—but no more. Today's kids are too smart for that old trick. They KNOW you DON'T know!

Oh well, it's good for my humility to occasionally know I don't know. Only you, Lord, know all the answers—and all the questions. Thank you, Lord, for giving us all—students, teachers, and parents—questioning minds. It would be so boring if we didn't have questions, if we didn't still yearn to learn, if we didn't still have wonder and wonderment. Help me to answer their questions—not just with information but also with inspiration. Help me to know when they are seeking MORE than the question implies, when they have a hidden agenda that needs to be explored, when they need a friend as much as a teacher.

And help me also, Lord, to decipher when they are just asking questions to stall, to put off work, to act smart-alecky. Give me patience and wisdom then to try to turn the smart-alecky into smart.

And if all else fails, Lord, I'll just respond to an unanswerable question by telling them to look up the anther!

~16~ Why does a head having a good hair day get more attention than a head full of knowledge?

Have you noticed, Lord, that most of the people on TV have heads that never have a bad hair day? And they also have heads decorated with perfect smiles and straight teeth? Is that why children are apt to believe everything those heads say?

It seems as if a "head" with good hair could suddenly decide to walk sideways like a crab and soon there would be children all over the country doing the crab-walk. A straight-teeth head could hold a press conference and pronounce that bilge water is good for the complexion and bilge water would suddenly become the drink of choice for youth.

Why is it, Lord, that a teacher or parent whose head has been well-educated and is filled with important life experiences cannot get that same kind of respect or attention?

Why are these children willing to believe ANYTHING told or sold on TV, but cannot accept the simplest truth from someone who really knows what he or she is talking about?

When television was first discovered, the pioneers envisioned it being a fabulous teaching tool. And it has been just that. Unfortunately, it has taught all the wrong things. What began as a beautiful dream has literally turned into a nightmare.

Forgive our culture, Lord, for allowing this to happen. Strengthen our backbones so we can fight this influence. People keep saying that if you don't like TV, just turn it off. But that's like saying if the air is polluted, just stop breathing.

The influence of TV has become so pervasive, it determines how we talk, what we wear, and even how we judge right from wrong!

Children spend more time with TV than doing anything else—except possibly sleeping! And statistics show that since the advent of television, violence and immorality have spread like a plague. Help us, Lord, to fight this.

Help us to turn off the soaps and wash out our minds instead. Help us to turn off the talk shows and take more time to talk with friends and family. Remind us to write sponsors and stations, demanding better programs. Teach us to be selective.

Help us to do all these things, Lord, so that we can set a good example for the children. You and I both know, Lord, that those children DO look to us for leadership— whenever we can get them to STOP looking at TV!

~17~ If it's so easy to criticize, why is it so hard to praise?

The words roll off my tongue like Uncle Ed sliding down a muddy riverbank!

You are so stupid.

You are so lazy.

You are so mindless, so careless, so thoughtless.

You never do what you are told.

You never pay attention.

You never remember ANYTHING!

If it's so easy to criticize, Lord, why is it so hard to praise? Help me, Lord, to shift my words from condemn to commend.

How can I expect these children to respond eagerly to my outstanding leadership if they are always flinching from my outstanding attacks?

Surely I can find SOMETHING nice to say about even the surliest and unruliest. I could start small, using just a few words and leaving out the last part of what I'm thinking.

You have a very special nickname (although Moonglow would not have been MY first choice) ... Your ideas are so interesting (AND unfathomable! What ARE you thinking?) … Blue is your best color (and it's a good thing since you're always starting fights) … You have such a nice voice (but you're going to wear it out if you keep talking ALL the time).

I'm not doing too good, am I, Lord? Maybe I better stick to things like "Your eyebrows are so even … your zip code is so easy to remember … your shoes match …" No, no, it's getting worse. You can see that I need to be tutored in "praise."

Wash my mouth out, Lord. Take away the bitter taste and fill it with your sweet compassion, your generosity—and kindness.

~18~ I never met Madame Curie
but we came up with the
same formula

Chemistry was always a mystery to me. Foaming chemicals and potions, observations and calculations, a laboratory filled with strange beakers and bottles—no, no, that field of study did not fit my prescription for success. But I was fascinated nevertheless by Madame Curie.

She was a heroine, an adventurer, a discoverer, a woman ahead of her time. But I had no idea we had anything in common until I recently came across a Curie quotation. Marie Curie said, "One never notices what has been done; one can only see what remains to be done."

Was she looking over my shoulder or what? Was her lifestyle then so much like mine now? Did the people in her world fail to notice the mopped floor, the completed report, the experiment in progress and say, "Do you mean you STILL haven't found time to answer that letter?" Oh yes, Lord, Marie knew just how I feel. Even a famous chemist cannot find a formula for doing it ALL.

No matter how much I do, no one notices. They only notice the un-done things I missed. Well, Lord, I know you understand how I feel. You do so much for all of us and we keep expecting more. We forget to thank you for all the blessings and only complain about the prayers you haven't answered in the way we expected.

You and Marie and I understand, Lord. We know that no matter how much is already done, there is still much to do. And maybe that's a good formula after all.

~19~ Who says it's a "social evil" to be alone?

Lord, remember when the Roman statesman Cato said: "Never am I less alone than when I am by myself; never am I more active than when I do nothing." Sure you remember, Lord! I don't remember but I read about it—and I agree!

Have you noticed how society thinks today's children must constantly be programmed to be with others? Kids just HAVE to go to every activity on the school calendar, participate in every after-school program, take music lessons, dance lessons, karate lessons, and attend every Little League game. ALL those things are good, Lord, but too much of a good thing can be too much!

Some children are seldom alone, always busy with activities away from home because there's no adult at home to be with them. Other children are alone too much, but it's a frightening unproductive aloneness because they are by themselves with no adult supervision. So I worry, Lord, about the children never having a safe, secure time of their own when they are free to be alone with their own thoughts and with you.

Some children need to be TAUGHT how to be alone because they have never had the opportunity or felt the desire. That's where I come in, Lord. Help me to teach them that being alone does not have to mean being lonely. Being alone can be the only way to learn who you are, what you want to be, where you want to go—and how to get there. Help me to teach the children to appreciate Cato's lesson, "Never am I less alone than when I am by myself."

~20~ I'm o.k., you're o.k.— but is that o.k.?

Today, Lord, we are constantly told to build up a child's self-image and that is certainly important. But what if we keep saying, "You're O.K.," and the kid knows that's not true? OR what if we say "You're O.K.," and don't mean it? Children have that uncanny knack of seeing through our words. They can almost always tell when we're saying something we don't really believe.

Help us, Lord, to look before we speak. Help us to find out what's happening with a child who might NOT be O.K. and try to fix what's wrong instead of just glossing over it. You can cover up a little sore with a bandage but underneath, it's still a sore—and it might even get worse if you don't apply the right medicine. You can never ONLY cover up a problem.

So help us, Lord, to take the time to get to KNOW what's happening with each child before we say, "You're O.K." It won't help them OR us to pretend things are all right when they're really all wrong.

We were all made in YOUR image, Lord. Help us to

remember that. Help us to live lives that will truly reflect YOUR image. Only then can we build up our own self-images—and show children how to build theirs. Only then can we say "I'm O.K., you're O.K."

~21~ I didn't plan to fail but I failed to plan

Lord, if I was going to drive to the next big city over the weekend, I would plan the trip. I would gas up the car and get a map to figure out what roads to take. I would decide what kind of clothes I would need and pack a suitcase. I might even bring a sack lunch.

And I would figure out how long it would take me to get there. But before I could do any of that, I would first have to consider where I AM.

Why is it so hard to teach children the skill of reflection and preparation? A boy decides he is going to be a doctor but he never plans to take any biology courses—they're too hard. A girl wants to be a concert pianist but she will only practice when there's nothing MORE IMPORTANT to do. They don't see the need for a map or a plan. They just expect to arrive where they want to go some day.

Am I that way too, Lord? Do I wonder why my plans fail when I should really be wondering why I failed to plan?

Do I expect to achieve goals faster than possible because I have not considered how far back I was when I started?

Oh dear Lord. The children and I sure have a lot in common, don't we? Well, at least that SHOULD make it easier for us to learn together and grow together. But first, we've got to get a plan!

~22~ Why do I always think of the perfect answer as soon as it is too late to give it?

Don't you just love the simple little things children ask, Lord? If gravity pulls down, why do we grow up? Do cows dream? Why is grass green instead of blue? And do frogs bump their bottoms when they hop?

Sometimes I can think of really great answers to questions like those, Lord—but it's always the next day or the next week or in the middle of the night. Why is that, Lord?

My mother used to tell me that I was usually a day late and a dollar short and I sure seem to be proving her right. Come to think of it, she always had good answers for my questions. Why didn't I inherit that facility? Of course, she could also sew beautifully and make fancy decorated cakes and play the piano and I can't do any of those things either. My genes don't seem to fit. But then neither do my jeans. But that's another story.

Help me, Lord, to have better responses to the children who look to me for answers. Even better, show me how to guide them to look for their OWN answers. And, Lord, please don't ever let me be abrupt or too busy to listen to their questions. Don't let me discourage them from asking because I know that if you stop asking and searching, that's when you get stuck in a rut and miss out on all the excitement of the continuing journey to tomorrow.

But speaking of questions reminds me, Lord—I have a few questions for you. Gotta minute?

~23~ Here we go again— another fire drill!

I got fired today, Lord. No, I didn't lose my job. I got fired UP—with ambition, enthusiasm, zeal, and foolishness. It looks like working with and for these children is going to be a lifetime sentence. Once even one child gets under your skin, you are attached for life.

I don't know how or why it happened, and it may not last long—but it's great while it lasts. Today, Lord, I'm ready to conquer the world. Tomorrow I may feel it has conquered me—but TODAY it is mine! I'm off on another fire drill!

Why is that, Lord? Why is it that some days, I am so with

it—in more ways than one? And other days, I am washed up, used up, and fed up? Some days I race like a greyhound. Other days I am like a turtle, inching along, dragging my house full of troubles wherever I go, making little progress, and pulling in my head every time somebody speaks to me.

You did this to me, Lord. You made me this way. But maybe it was because you knew that once I got fired up, I would burn in all directions at once, using up my fuel supply in a wanton display of activity. And then I would NEED that downtime to refuel and recharge the batteries.

Thank you, Lord, for the up days and the down days. Help me to make the most of both—using the fiery ones to entertain and educate the children with a blaze of creativity, using the embered ones to teach them the value of quiet time. But can't talk any longer, Lord. Gotta go—while I'm all fired up!

~24~ Flying by the skin of your knuckles

According to Chinese legend, a mandarin once tried to fly by hanging from two paper kites driven by a lot of rockets. I sure hope these kids don't hear about that!

It's amazing, Lord, how kids will try anything once—and sometimes twice! Then they grow up and get more cautious and miss out on a lot of adventures, as well as a lot of fractures.

Lord, why do adults so quickly turn into white knuckle travelers? Those who once broke into song just for the fun of it will no longer be seen singing in public, even in church! Those who once journeyed forth on flights of fancy now want seat belts on their armchairs. Those who once marveled at the mysteries of your rain forests and daffodils now have eyes only for time clocks and paychecks.

Well, Lord, we all have to grow up some time I guess, but please help us adults to remember what it was like to be a child and child-like. When a child comes to us—wide-eyed with wonder—remind us to not turn away because we're too busy to be surprised and excited. When a child comes to us—crying over a lost pencil or a postponed picnic—remind us how big those small losses can seem to small children.

You do ALL of that, Lord, when we come to you, eager to share our small wonders or crying over our own small losses. And you have so many more children to care for than we do. Thank you, Lord, for listening. Help us to be as generous.

~25~ If barbed wire keeps people out, what about barbed words?

Did the person who invented barbed wire intend for it to keep something out or in, Lord? Was it planned to keep the unwanted people out or the wanted people in?

Whichever it was, it works either way. But barbed words work only one way. They keep others OUT.

You might hope barbed words could fence a family in or keep students cooped in a classroom. But barbs HURT so much they are only effective in keeping away instead of drawing in.

Lord, please help me to de-barb my words, to never speak to children—OR to adults—with the INTENTION of hurting. Sometimes my run-away mouth might speak before my brain has given it the proper instruction—and hurt unintentionally. But please, Lord, teach me to never barb on purpose.

I keep thinking of that wise prayer, "Keep my words sweet today, Lord, for tomorrow I may have to eat them." You and I both know, Lord, how often I have been served yesterday's words on a plate of embarrassment or chagrin. Forgive me, Lord, for my haste. Slow my motor mouth. Replace the sharp spikes with gentleness and giggles.

Help me to learn how to speak so that children will feel they are wanted in, not shut out. Turn my conversation into a safe harbor—instead of barbed garbage!

~26~ Who turned off the brights?

A wise lady once told me, "If there is no bright side, polish up the dark one." Wouldn't we be bright, Lord, if we could all remember that every day?

The media reminds us constantly how dark the picture is, how bleak the present and the future are for children. We listen and sigh and wonder what WE can do to change things. Yet we know the answer. WE are the answer, the hope, the cure.

If the world has turned dark for children, it is only the adults who have the power to polish it up. So help us, Lord, to get started NOW before any more clouds come along!

It isn't possible for one person to change the big picture overnight but it IS possible for each of us to try to polish up the picture in our immediate vicinity.

That old saying about lighting one candle instead of cursing the darkness is more valid than ever. Help us pass out those candles, Lord. Today's children were not made to be drug addicts, prison inmates, or other such losers. They were made in your image and it's our job to get them polished up so others will recognize them for who they truly are.

It's a big job, Lord—too big for one person, one city, one state, or one nation. But, like all jobs, it has to start with one. So help us, Lord, to find brave and wise leaders to follow. And help us to keep polishing the dark sides and turning the brights back on!

~27~ Tramp, tramp, tramp; my feet are flattening and my arches are falling

My eyes see the glory and the joy, Lord, but my feet hurt! They're tired of carrying the weight of my world day and night. They're too used-up to keep up with this hop, skip, and jump. Children's feet and legs have built-in springs but my springs have sprung.

Lord, I know nature walks, camp-outs, and hiking woodland trails are good for teaching many lessons. But the lesson they've taught me is that my feet are flattening and my arches are falling. These little piggies need rest, soak, and balm, Lord.

But I know there's another lesson here to be learned. I must walk more closely with others who share my task of leading and teaching. Only those who have been in the same shoes can understand the problems, the sorrows, the possibilities. We should stand together, swapping stories and solutions, comparing and consoling. I need that, Lord—and I know others do too.

Help me, Lord, to reach out to others—being gracious enough to offer my support and concern and being un-ashamed to ask for theirs in return. No matter how wonderfully talented and creative and self-motivated I am, I realize I cannot walk alone.

When my spirits sag and my feet flag, I know I can count on you, Lord. But today, I also need a human voice, a human hand, a human hug. So, Lord, could you please send someone along my footpath to massage my psyche—AND my aching feet?

~28~ I wish I had said that!

Words. I love a good quotation, Lord. Mark Twain said, "The difference between the almost-right word and the right word is … the difference between the lightning bug and the lightning." And Shakespeare said, "Eye of newt and toe of frog, wool of bat, and tongue of dog."

Well, I might have said that last one, Lord. I've said similar words when I've stubbed my toe in the dark of night or heard the alarm in the dark of morning. But, Lord, I'd like to be able to come up with the "right" words at the "right" times.

Most of all, I'd like to be able to fire off some clever comebacks to those kids AND adults who frequently hit me with a zinger or a stinger. Oh, I usually think of some appropriately (and often diabolically) clever retort—but not until an hour later, a day later, or the next year. Why is that, Lord? Why does my brain go on flight-delay and become temporarily out of service?

Well, maybe it's a good thing, Lord. There is a natural barb in my tongue and it could do a lot of damage if it ever got loose on time and on target. It's probably best that I only think of those sharp retorts long later when I am stewing alone.

Thanks, Lord, for keeping me from being mean by saying what I mean. Thank you for forcing me to think twice before I speak.

~29~ When I pass go, why can't I collect $200?

Whew! I got it all done, Lord. The books are put away, the room straightened, the phone calls made, the schedules drawn up for next week, the plans for Tuesday's meeting formulated, the materials ready for Wednesday's project. I think I'm all finished. Now what do I do next? Oh yes, I remember. Start over!

Why is that, Lord? Why is it that when I finish, I'm never finished. There's always another day with new problems to solve and more putting away, straightening, planning, and catching up. I keep passing GO but I never collect $200. All I seem to collect is dust—and whines.

Forgive my whining, Lord. Thank you for the opportunity to teach, to plan, to schedule, to be active and productive. I know there are many who have a much more difficult life, many who would love to trade for mine, many who would think I am the luckiest of all people. And I think that too some days, Lord. I know I should think that most EVERY day.

Thank you, Lord, for all my blessings. There are a few pockmarks and potholes in my life but there have been a lot more green lights than stop signs. And I am grateful. Help me to pass on an attitude of gratitude to the children. Help me to show them that in spite of whatever trouble they have, they too are blessed. They too are loved by you—and by me.

~30~ Stop the world, this is my station

Some wiseacre said that it is easy to find your station in life: Sooner or later, someone will tell you where to get off!

Well, a lot of people have told me that, Lord, and I've gotten off—and then on again—and then off again. But somehow, I always end up on the Streetcar Named Require.

I'm always assigned some task that requires more training, more research, more time. And of course, none of this ever leads to more money—but let's not talk about that just now.

Lord, some days I feel I have arrived at a very high station—what could be more important than dispensing knowledge and guidance to children? Other days I feel my station is very low—but on those days, I realize that if it is as bad as I think, there is nowhere to go but up. Of course, going up requires not standing still or remaining stationary.

Speaking of that, I better get going, Lord. I have work to do and if I don't get with it, there are several people lining up at my station, just waiting to tell me where to get off!

~31~ Who ever told children snakes could be your friends?

Why is it, Lord, that children are always curious about things that are best left alone? Did you put magnets in their dear little heads that just draw them to mud puddles, sticky chewing gum, and spiders, snakes, and other crawly things?

Why do authors and illustrators fill their children's books with friendly snakes like a four-foot slimy-looking boa constrictor cleverly named Noah the Boa or Julius Squeezer? Why did Charlotte have to be such a wonderful weaver and role model?

When I was a child, you must have forgotten my magnet, Lord. Creepy, crawly things do not fill me with glee. They fill me with terror! I don't want to even look at one, much less touch it, let it sit on my hand, or curl around my arm. Yuck!

Yet here I am with these children on field trips, trying to act calm and cool, trying to not let them know that the adult who is "in charge" may, at any moment, run in panic for the nearest exit!

You must have had your reasons, Lord, for making these strange creatures—just like you had your reasons for making strange people like me. And I do find it interesting that you gave bugs all those feet while I only have two and you gave snakeskin all those patterns and designs while my skin has no pattern at all except for some wrinkles in all the wrong places. But I would find it even more interesting to READ about those things without having to see them up close. Could you PLEASE arrange it, Lord, so that I could go only on field trips to the museum while somebody else shows the kids the snake pits?

~32~ Why doesn't the pursuit of happiness come with a map?

I understand I've got the right to life, liberty, and the pursuit of happiness! Big deal. Scavenger hunts can be fun, but pursuing and never finding can be harmful to your health. Where is my map, Lord?

As I struggle to lead the children in the right direction, I keep going down dead-end streets, off the beaten paths, up the road less traveled—and where does it get me? I have to admit it's been interesting pursuing happiness, but now I want to find it, catch it, roll in it!

Lord, I know you are supposed to enjoy the journey instead of just what comes at the end of the line. I have had a lot of fun along the way. My crooked byways were often more exciting than many people's smooth highways. It's just that on days like this, Lord, I tend to sag and droop.

I forget all the treasures the children and I have discovered on the detours and I remember only the potholes. I get tired of always traveling tourist and yearn for a first-class ticket.

Forgive me, Lord. And thanks for the smiles along the miles. But, Lord, if you DO happen to come across one of those road maps that gives directions and rest stops, please send it my way. I've been trying to do the best I can with just hints and innuendoes—today I need DIRECTIONS!

~33~ It's about time!

Oh Lord, WHY did you give children a different concept of time than the one you gave to adults? When children have to WAIT, time stands still. They can't imagine why it is taking YOU so long to get what THEY want. But when YOU are in a hurry and only have a few minutes to finish a project or a chore, they are in no hurry at all. They act as if you both have all the time in the world.

When children are late, they can't understand why you are so upset. When YOU are late, they can't understand what took you so long. Adults and children live in different time zones even when they are in the same room.

Well, Lord, I guess we ALL live in a different time zone than you do. We pray for something and expect you to give it to us NOW. After all, we only have a few years here on earth to get things done. But YOU have eternity. No wonder you can't understand why we're in such a hurry.

Give us patience, Lord—patience to put up with the way children view time AND with the way you view it! But, Lord, you know I've been praying for that one special intention a very long time now. Could you please put a rush on it? Could you please give me an answer soon? I think it's about time!

What do you think?

~34~ Faster than a speeding bullet—the super-me syndrome

My cape isn't working today, Lord. My superness is having a superiority crisis. Sure, I learned long ago—as anyone does who deals with children—how to move faster than a speeding bullet. But you and I both know, Lord, that I'll never be as powerful as a locomotive. And I can't leap tall problems in a single bound.

Today is worse than usual, Lord. The S on my chest does not stand for Super. It stands for SCARED.

I am so scared. I feel so small, so stupid, so vulnerable, so needy. I have been pumping myself up, pretending I could do it all—be all things to all people. Who was I kidding, Lord?

Today I had to face facts. I can only do so much. I cannot expect to work wonders, only work. I cannot expect to make big changes, only little ones. I cannot expect to be a Super Me, only the real me.

Everything went wrong today, Lord. The kid I thought I was helping showed me I wasn't. The child I thought was making real progress proved to me he wasn't. And then the heel broke off my shoe.

My Super Status is sinking low, Lord. Has someone been sneaking Kryptonite into my coffee? Or am I the one who has been trying so hard to be perfect that I didn't have enough time left over to be real?

Forgive me, Lord. Remind me that I don't have to be a Super Me. I just have to be the best me I can be. And I can do that, Lord, if you'll just help me stay out of those telephone booths!

~35~ Mary, Harry, quite contrary, how does your garden grow?

There's a story about a man who said to his gardener, "Plant this tree tomorrow." The gardener replied, "Do you realize it won't bear fruit for a hundred years?" And the man said, "Then you better plant it today!"

We criticize children, Lord, for wanting everything NOW and yet we adults are just as guilty. We plant a seed of knowledge in their little brains and want it to sprout forth NOW. Deep down, we know it could take months or even years before that seed sprouts, blossoms, and bears fruit. But we don't want to admit that. We hate to face that possibility. We allow ourselves to get discouraged while we wait.

Give us patience, Lord. Help us to value the experience of watching each child grow at a different pace. Help us to be aware and to praise each little greening bud as it appears so that each child will know we value his or her growth of knowledge, no matter how small or how far below our expectations.

It's hard, Lord, to keep it up, to continually encourage and to nourish, especially when we see so little progress. It's hard to know how to praise small efforts and yet at the same time convince the children not to settle for small but to keep trying harder to reach that next rung, to aspire to do better. It's hard to accept—and teach—that every child can't be best but each CAN do better.

It's hard, Lord, but we must do it. I must do it. Help me to plant the tree, fertilize and water and envelop it with my sunshine of understanding—and then wait.

~36~ And the winner is …

Aren't awards wonderful, Lord? Or are they? A wit says an award is more a reflection of those presenting it than those receiving it. And sometimes it is.

Sometimes it seems organizations give awards just so they will have an excuse to have an award dinner and get some free publicity. Sometimes it seems schools give awards just so the recipient can say, "See what I got" and make others wish they had one too. And sometimes the very ones who SHOULD receive awards remain unrewarded.

What about awards for plumbers, electricians, butchers, grocery clerks, auto mechanics, or Great Aunt Sue? Could we—or would we want to—live without such folk? I think not. And yet we thank and award them too seldom.

And we also give them too little respect. Help us, Lord, to teach children that there is dignity in all work. Help us to encourage them in whatever career they choose, and remind them that you don't have to have a prestigious professional career to do worthwhile work.

We all long for the awards and recognition of the world, Lord. Help us see that what we SHOULD long for is not of this world. Help us teach the children, Lord, that leading a simple, good, moral life really is all the reward we need.

~37~ Everybody's got my number!

I used to have a name. Now I have a number. I am not a hot number but I am defined by numbers. I have zip and area code numbers. I have telephone, credit card, ATM, and social security numbers. I dare not forget a single digit because, Lord, my days are numbered.

Maybe that wouldn't be so bad but now those kids have got my number too!

I've tried to fool them into thinking I know everything. It worked for a while but then they got suspicious! Now they've got my number.

What are we going to do about that, Lord? Yes, I know. I have to work harder, smile more, make learning more exciting (for all of us!), try new ideas, resurrect old ideas, and pray a lot!

Then I can count my blessings—which are numberless—and teach the children how to count theirs.

And when my countless friends are unavailable when I need advice about how to teach or how to count, I can always call you, Lord. I know you'll answer because you're the only one left who doesn't have an answering machine or an unlisted number!

~38~ Isn't that red light ever going to change?

I guess you've seen me, Lord, racing to that light on the corner. As I come over the hill, it is always green and I race to make it but then it changes to red JUST before I get there. My brakes screech to a halt and I sit there, fuming, complaining that if I'm late, it will be the fault of that stupid light.

But you know, Lord, one day I timed that light. It took forty-two seconds to change. Forty-two seconds! I spend more time than that stirring the cream into my coffee or making faces in the mirror to see if my eyebrows are still working.

Obviously, Lord, I've uncovered another virtue that needs practice. So give me patience, Lord—but hurry.

Just a generation ago, Lord, children were taught the names of all the virtues and urged to practice them. If you asked some of them about virtue today, they'd answer it could be the name of a rock star or maybe a new yogurt flavor.

Ah yes, the world has changed and as it has, impatience has become THE virtue: hurry up so you won't get left behind, run faster or the world will pass you by, speed it up or you'll lose the rat race. Sorry, Lord—it looks like I'm one of the guilties.

Hold me back and keep me from passing on this urge to hurry. Lead me to teach the children how to work at a steady pace instead of in a frenetic panic. Give me—and give them—the ability to wait patiently through the red lights of life, having faith that soon you will turn the red to green. And now I know, Lord, that sometimes you do that in only forty-two seconds!

~39~ To scheme the impossible scheme

"She didn't know it couldn't be done so she did it." How often I think of that sentence, Lord. It has inspired me to scheme impossible schemes.

I envy the innocence of small children who haven't learned yet about the idea of impossibility. It's harder for us older folk who have tried and failed, who have aimed high and been shot down. It's harder to keep trying again, to keep going out on that limb, wondering if it will get sawed off. But when I start wavering, I remember that inspiring sentence and start scheming.

Thank you, Lord, for the irrepressibility of children. Watching that spirit of "try anything, do anything" can encourage us to get up and get going again—but it can also scare us silly. Those kids are often so undaunted, they tempt danger. So help us, Lord, to learn from them the lesson of do-ability—and help us teach them the lesson of care-fulness.

Give us, Lord, the gullibility to try and the grit to try again. And thank you, Lord, for setting such a good example, for being such a good teacher. It has been rumored that you made the whole world in just seven days. Now THAT was an impossible scheme!

~40~ How do we cross that fine line between tune-in and turn-off?

I've been getting a lot of static on my broadcasting system, Lord. I keep sending out messages but instead of those children being tuned in, they are turned off. How can I get them to pick up my signals?

Oh, sure, I forgot. You have that same problem don't you? We are often too busy or too preoccupied or too lazy or too self-centered to tune-in or turn-on to your miracles.

George Washington Carver said, "I love to think of nature as an unlimited broadcasting system through which God speaks to us every hour, if we will only tune in." How wonderful, Lord, to think that we are surrounded with your nature, your voice, your reassurance, your love—and all we have to do is tune in to receive it.

Help me, Lord, to pass on this message to the children. They understand tuning in. They don't seem to be able to live more than a few minutes without constant noise—music, videos, video games, TV, radio, or a telephone super-glued to the ear. I should be able to explain to them that radio and TV stations do not stop broadcasting when they change the dial. The signal is still there but they will miss it if they don't tune-in or turn-on—just as YOUR signal, your message, is always there, waiting for us to receive it.

And, Lord, if I can help them turn-on to YOU, could you please help them to turn-on to ME too?

~41~ I gotta get more exercise!

They say the mind is a muscle and it has to be exercised and stretched to stay current. It has to be pushed and prodded to perform properly. So I guess that's why my mind feels real flabby sometimes and other times gets all worn out from jogging all day to keep up with those kids.

It's obvious, Lord, that I need a more efficient exercise program. I've gotta learn how to run in place, use proper I.Q. equipment, and get in condition to flex, spring, and catapult.

Help me, Lord, to keep up my enthusiasm for learning so I can pass it on. Help me to continue to find joy in exploring why in the world, how in the world, and what in the world happened when. Help me to get excited about amazing facts and the strangest stories ever told. And help me to share their delight when the kids start to pass on even more of those stories to me than I can pass on to them!

Oh, Lord, learning is so much fun. It's one kind of exercise I really like. Maybe that's because it's the only kind of exercise I can do without letting 'em see me sweat!

But, Lord, you know they say that not only is the mind a muscle, it's also like a parachute. That's because it only works right if it opens. Help me, Lord, to show the children how to open their minds and exercise them too. But help me to also show them how important it is to use discipline, both in exercise and sky diving, so they will always fly with you and have a safe landing.

~42~ Running in high gear does not put you in the driver's seat

Have you noticed, Lord, how some people don't care where they're going just as long as they're in the driver's seat? Have I been like that, Lord?

Have I been so busy trying to be IN CONTROL that I didn't see where I was going, didn't notice the detour or the dead-end signs? Have I been unconsciously challenging the children, daring them to outrun me, when I should have noticed that we were due for a collision?

Lord, I know that children and adults are always struggling for control, racing in high gear, determined to outsmart each other. But I'm the adult. I should be the one to realize when it's time to put on the brakes.

I'm the one who should admit that only one can be in control and that one is YOU. Forgive me, Lord. Help me to slow down and smell the tire burns. Remind me that children are not robots to be programmed and controlled but lovable human beings to be taught and guided. Let me recognize when it is important to establish my control AND when it is just as important to shift into idle for a while and prayerfully try the REMOTE control.

Teach me how to hold tight with open hands.

~43~ They never promised me a rose garden

When I first got involved with kids, Lord, I had this beautiful picture in my head of a garden of small smiling faces, lifting their heads to the sun, bobbing happily in perfect unison, thriving and blossoming and maturing into perfection. Who put all these weeds in my garden?

Sorry, Lord, I know none of the children are weeds—they are just weedy LOOKING. And maybe that's because they are so needy. No one told me it was going to be easy—I just hoped it would be. I was wrong.

I have learned that you can't go somewhere and BUY a bouquet of beautiful cut flowers and then dig a hole and stick them in it and expect them to grow and turn into a garden. No. You have to take a packet of ugly little seeds and plant them with loving care and then water and fertilize and tend and talk to them. Oh so gradually, they will grow—but not always into the perfect garden you had planned.

Help me, Lord, to keep on digging. Draw my eye to the ones that are wilting and need a little extra attention. Help me restrain the ones that are showy and want to take over and push down the others. Keep me alert since just a little neglect can cause the growth to slow down and the blossoming to falter.

And thank you, Lord, for letting me work with these little seedlings. Help me to grow with them. And help me remember that you can't have a rose garden without a few thorns!

~44~ When did stuff become more important than "the right stuff"?

There was a time—not so long ago—when a person described as "having the right stuff" was a person who had integrity, honor, courage, and stick-to-itiveness. Today a person with good "stuff" is a person who has all the latest and most expensive "toys"!

Lord, how did this happen? How did young people start believing that the most important thing in life is to have the "best" music system, the latest video game, and the kind of clothes "to die for"—but things like honor and integrity are just words that have nothing to do with being a TODAY person?

And look at me, Lord. I want to be a today person too! I want to have all the good stuff—even though I know down deep that none of that matters a hoot. And sometimes I have to dig down pretty deep to remind myself!

But, Lord, I also know that "things" are not bad in themselves. I know you don't mind if I build a snug nest for myself and decorate it with a few treasures—like the family photos and that cherished mirror I found at a garage sale years ago. I just have to remember to not let possessions possess me. And I have to pass on that knowledge to the children.

So, Lord, please help me to have the integrity and honor and courage and stick-to-itiveness to teach today's youth to quit stuffing their lives with stuff and to work instead to possess the right stuff!

~45~ Why the best plans often do not turn out as planned

I had it all planned, Lord. The whole day. It was so efficient, so organized, so intelligent. What happened?

I don't want to talk about the unscheduled schedule shuffle that threw off my timetable, the unexpected thunderstorm that exploded my plan for an outdoor learning experience, or the unannounced surprise visit by that "very important person." And I don't want to even think about the child who suddenly got the hiccups right in the middle of my carefully prepared, well-thought-out lesson. Who can listen or talk or think while waiting expectantly for the next hiccup to hic!

No, Lord, I don't want to talk about any of that. What I want to talk about is you—and how you keep turning my lessons for others into lessons for ME! Yes, Lord, I learned my lesson.

I learned that I must be more flexible so that simple disturbances will not disturb me so much; I must be prepared but also ready to adapt; I must remain in control when things happen that are beyond my control AND beyond the control of the perpetrator—like the hiccup-pee.

I must remember that sometimes "suffering is resistance to what is." Instead of resisting every small change of my "plans" and therefore "suffering" through them, I must try to accept "what is" and make the most of it. Maybe I could even learn to laugh at such things when they happen—instead of a year later when I'm remembering them. That isn't an easy lesson to learn, Lord, but I'm willing to try.

~46~ Look out, there's a sponge in the room!

Who would have ever believed—except you, Lord—that some day civilized people would use a skeleton to wash up the dishes, wash out the bathtub, and wash off little fingerprints from walls! Yes, Lord, only you could have thought to invent something as strange as a sponge. Now, of course, we civilized people can make synthetic sponges so we don't have to feel guilty any more about using the skeleton of a marine mammal's deceased relative to do our dirty work!

Today I was sitting around thinking about sponges and how they are so good for sopping up and how children are so much like them. The only problem with children, Lord, is that they sop up good AND bad. That's why we have to be so careful what we say or do or teach because they will sop it all up indiscriminately.

It's so easy to squeeze out a sponge and get rid of all the dirty water but it's not that easy to squeeze out the mind of a child once it has sopped up an idea.

Help me, Lord, to always try to act, speak, and react properly when children are present. Keep me aware and alert. Those darling little sponges are watching my every move and ready to sop at the drop of an idea or a slip of the lip.

~47~ Do I spend more time cleaning out my closet than I do cleaning out that idea file in my head?

Once in a blue moon, Lord, I get up enough energy to clean out a closet or a basement. I am always amazed at what I find. Sometimes I wonder why I saved all that junk! I fill up waste baskets with stuff to pitch and boxes with other stuff to give away. But I also find treasures!

I come across a pair of warm wool gloves or an almost-new shirt I had totally forgotten. And I am delighted to be able to wear them again—kind of like renewing an old friendship. I find snapshots I had stashed away and thought lost forever. And I am delighted to stick them in the album where they belong. Even though I put it off as long as possible, cleaning out can be a chore with a happy ending.

So why don't I take some time to clear out that stuff filed away in my head—old ideas that are no longer good ideas, old plans that are no longer possible or even desirable, old dreams that should be replaced with new ones. And who knows, I might find some treasure there too! I might find usable ideas or plans or dreams. I might find things that once made me happy but have been shoved to the back, waiting for me to rediscover.

Yes, Lord, I should definitely clean out my closets and my

idea file more often. How can I teach children to be tidy if I don't set a good example? How can I teach them how important it is to know when to throw away and when to keep—unless I practice what I teach? Help me, Lord, to be more discerning in cleaning, pitching, saving—and recognizing a treasure when I find one!

~48~ Can getting a handle on things lead to the exit?

I've got it all together now. I've found the secret of the universe, Lord. I've just learned that the word "helve" means the handle of a hammer.

Now that I've got a handle on things, will this lead me to turn it and open the door to new vistas—or just to follow the exit sign?

But wait, there's more. I also learned that "actothorp" is the word for the # sign on a telephone and "fillip" is what you call the snapping sound you make with your thumb and middle finger like when you say, "That's it! I've got it!"

Why am I telling you these things, Lord? You already know them! But then I'm always telling you things you already know. And you just smile and nod and nictitate (which I also learned means "wink").

Thank you, Lord, for being so kind and patient with me. Help me to return the favor by being kind and patient when the children tell me long stories about things they've just discovered—but I already knew. Remind me to smile and nod and widen my eyes in surprise and then nictitate conspiratorially as though we are the only ones in the universe to share such startling knowledge.

Help me to be as good a listener to others as you have been to me, Lord. You are a good role model!

~49~ If the best things in life are free, why am I in the red?

Yes, I am seeing red today, Lord. And it's not just in my checkbook. I'm not only broke, I'm mad too. I see so many children getting a free ride, causing free-for-alls, and demanding freedom for themselves while TAKING it from others. And I know they got these ideas from the adults in charge!

Where will it all end, Lord? Will we ever be free of all this free talk? Will we ever again hear such words as responsibility, independence, or hard work?

I know the idea of being free is exhilarating and alluring. I have felt it. I have known it. But I know also that it's an idea that can imprison those who demand it.

Children who believe the world owes them a living must learn that the best kind of living is one that has been earned. They must be taught that there are two sides to the coin—freedom on one side, responsibility on the other. Too many of today's children have never even considered that.

And it is our fault, Lord—the fault of today's media, today's parents, today's teachers, today's people-in-charge. It is the fault of people who should know better.

Help us, Lord, to change that thinking. You are the only one who gives us things that are free AND worthwhile. You give us life, sunshine, water, a brain, and a body. And then you give us the freedom to decide how to use them—wisely or NOT.

Help me, Lord, to teach the children that if you want a candy bar or an education, SOMEBODY has to work to pay for it!

~50~ Do I too often see without seeing?

Lord, today I was thinking about something I heard a long time ago. Some wise person said that each day you should take the time to stop and look at something in your world and say, "Isn't that *beautiful*?"

I know that the world at-large AND my private world runneth over with beautiful things, but it's so easy to take them for granted or to just not notice anymore. I speed along the highway, passing fields of rainbowed wildflowers; I hurry through a mall, not noticing the faces of those walking past; I race through an art museum, looking with one eye at the masterpieces because the other eye is busy checking to see what the children are touching that is untouchable.

I see without seeing.

I have allowed complexity and busy-ness to crowd into my life until there is too little room left for beauty. What a loss, what a shame.

I AM ashamed, Lord. When I take the time, I revel in the beauty of the world. I love to gather wildflowers, watch a waterfall, sit in a crowd and notice the amazing diversity of the faces you have made. But I too seldom take the time.

How can I gift children with the love of beauty if I do not cultivate it more in myself? Slow me down, Lord, so I can learn and then teach this lesson: At least once each day, let me stop to look closely at one of the wonders of this world and say, "Isn't that *beautiful*?"

~51~ Too much stick-to-itiveness can gum up things

It's a sticky subject, Lord, but I heard that someone recently discovered a nine thousand-year-old piece of chewing gum that still had teeth marks in it! I wonder if the gum was found stuck under a Stone Age school desk or on the leg of a cafeteria table. They probably didn't have either of those nine thousand years ago but they DID have kids—and where there's a kid, there's gum.

What is this fascination with chewing on flavored rubber, Lord? And why do kids insist on getting it stuck in or on everything they touch? Don't they know adults have better things to do than use scrapers and high pressure hoses to unglue their chew?

Well, I guess that's another of the many mysteries of childhood. They say the jaw power kids use to chew gum could light a city of ten million for a year! Wow! If only they would bite into education with as much enthusiasm!

I didn't mean to chew on this subject so long, Lord. I was just wondering why humans are the only creation of yours who like to chew gum. But then I wonder why humans are your only creation who do a lot of dumb things—like sitting around and THINKING about chewing gum!

Sorry, Lord. I should be thinking about more important things today—like how to get those kids to stop jawing about nothing and start discussing intellectual subjects like I do.

Hmmmm. Now where did I put that gum wrapper?

~52~ Now why didn't I think of that?

Some people are so creative, so ingenious, so imaginative—so irritating! How come THEY always think of the good ideas, the good answers, the innovative solutions to problems?

Sometimes their ideas are so SIMPLE—yet so perfect. They come up with such OBVIOUS things that work so well. How come THEY can so quickly see the solutions that others miss?

What am I doing wrong, Lord? I pray, I meditate, I search, I study. So why are THEY always the ones with the answers?

I'm tired of it, Lord. I'm tired of always standing around with my mouth hanging open and my eyes bulging out, wondering, "Now why didn't I think of that?"

Yes, Lord, I know. I should be grateful that SOMEBODY thinks of these things and I am fortunate enough to be around to take advantage of their ingenuity. At least, I'm not too proud to take notes AND take note of how I can apply what others discover. At least I'm smart enough to know how to steal an idea when I see one. So thank you, Lord, for that skill of mine. Keep putting me with those OTHER people who are so clever so I can take their brilliance and reflect it on the children I teach and touch.

And, Lord, thanks for the few times that I am the one who comes up with a bright idea. It's so nice to hear someone ELSE say, "Now why didn't I think of that?"

~53~ All work and no play— and still not enough hours in the day!

Twenty or thirty years ago, the futurists were predicting that we would soon have so many labor-saving devices, we would be FREE—free of boring chores, long workdays, and household drudgery. What went wrong, Lord?

Today career, family, and etceteras all add up to what sometimes seems like a twenty-four-hour workday! As soon as we began to get all those labor-saving devices, somebody devised reasons we should take on more and more duties.

What happened to all that leisure time our society was supposed to discover? How come I seldom find myself sitting in a lounge chair, watching the surf and the world roll by? Seldom? Who am I kidding? Nigh on to never!

Well, maybe it wouldn't be too good to have too much leisure time. Vacations are nice but they end. Teaching and learning, reaching and growing go on forever—and make life interesting.

But, Lord, we all know what ALL work and no play makes—and who wants to be dull? So please, Lord, help me to make proper use of my labor-saving devices so I can find time for some face-saving, brain-saving leisure.

Some surf and sun would be nice. Or maybe some turf

and shade, mountains in the moonlight, islands in the daylight. But I'm easy, Lord. I'll settle for an afternoon in the backyard with a good book and a glass of iced tea, no chores, and a few snores. How about it, Lord? Next Tuesday sound good?

~54~ Who decided role models are supposed to rock and roll?

My idea of a role model is a saint, a philanthropist, a wise teacher, a dedicated scientist searching to find a cure for a terrible disease. Children of today seem to have a different idea! They think a role model is a rock star or a sport's hero.

How did this happen, Lord? Who decided that a role model has to be somebody who is rolling in money and appears regularly on MTV or in shoe commercials?

When did people who play ball or make noise, excuse me, music, become people with all the answers? Sure, Super Bowls and maybe even rock concerts can be fun—but how far do they really go to make the world a better place?

Being a good parent, a good uncle or aunt, a good friend—or maybe being a good doctor, lawyer, or merchant chief—COULD make the world a better place. So why aren't they today's role models? Why aren't they the ones the youth admire and want to be like when they grow up?

There was a time when children went to movies or ballgames or listened to music and were entertained, but they didn't really EXPECT to some day have the same lifestyle as the entertainers. Some few dreamed of becoming celebrities and even fewer worked for it and achieved their dream. But most children expected to grow up to be like their parents or grandparents who worked hard to provide for the family, occasionally took time out for a picnic or outing in the country, and led a good but simple life.

Those days seem gone forever, Lord. Today too many kids actually believe life can be beautiful ONLY IF you grow up to live in a mansion, ride in a limo, take extended vacations to other continents, and make lots of money playing ball or starring in a soap opera. Some of them might—maybe one-tenth of one percent. But that leaves ninety-nine and nine-tenths without a limo!

Lord, Lord, why did you let "ordinary people" lose their place as heroes and heroines? Why did you let role models switch from substance to smoke? And how can we switch it back?

What's that you say? You say YOU didn't let it happen—we did? We ordinary people complained so much about our own lifestyles that the children decided they sure didn't want to be like us? Oh!

Well, maybe it's not too late! Help us ordinary people, Lord, to show the children that there's often fool's gold beneath the glitter of celebrity but there's REAL gold in simple, everyday family life. But please hurry, Lord. We've wasted lots of time. And those OTHER role models are really on a roll!

~55~ Lost and found or found and lost?

Lord, I need a personal, private Lost and Found for the things I keep losing—my temper, my good intentions, my car keys, and my train of thought. There's no doubt about it—I'm a loser.

Well, it could be worse. I could lose the will to live, old friends, new possibilities, or my credit card. I've still got all those, Lord, so who could ask for anything more?

Sometimes, Lord, I think we worry so much about our own big, important losses, we forget to pay enough attention to what seem like the trivial losses of others—especially those of children.

We think children can bounce back from anything. They're young, they're flexible, they'll outgrow it. But sometimes it's not as easy as we'd like to believe.

Thornton Wilder said, "Many who have spent a lifetime in it can tell us less of love than the child that lost a dog yesterday." Children may seem to bounce back quickly but they too feel pain, sometimes very deeply, sometimes too deeply.

Help me, Lord, to recognize their pain but to not try to take it away. Instead, help me to teach them to cope with it and work through it so it will not leave a permanent sting or stain.

Help me to teach them AND myself how to grieve over the lost and then let it go, how to rejoice over the found and treasure it but, if necessary, let it go too.

But, Lord, I sure wish I could find that lost train of thought. Where DID it go?

~56~ Can information lead to infirmation?

This is supposed to be the information age, Lord—but all this information is making me infirm. My back is crumbling from carrying around all the reading material that keeps crossing my desk, my eyes are fading from all of the late night catch-up. My brain has gone into overload. But I now know everything about everything I cannot do anything about!

Today there was an earthquake in some town I had trouble finding on the map, labor strikes in a remote region of a remote country, a maniac terrorizing a neighborhood with drive-by shootings—and those were just the topics in one segment of TV headline news.

Newspapers are filling my garage, books are stacked in my basement, computer printouts are straining the seams of my carryall, and all this input is straining the seams of my psyche!

Then people have the nerve to ask me if I read the Bible every day! How can I read the Bible when I have so many OTHER important things to read, scan, interiorize, memorize, and synthesize?

What's that you say? The Bible is the greatest story ever told, the best-selling book in history, and, oh-by-the-way, the inspired word of God? Hmmm ... maybe I could find ten minutes somewhere to give it a glance.

Just maybe that's the kind of information I've been needing to get me off the infirm list and onto the in-formation list!

Thanks, Lord, for your input!

~57~ Mod, funky, rad, grungy— like the fads, I'm fading fast

I used to speak English, Lord. I used to be able to communicate with other people—young and old—who I would see in the neighborhood, shopping centers, or at church. Now both young and old speak a different language than I do!

Even the latest dictionary accepts strange usage and lists such words and phrases as megabit, boom box, voice mail, and veg out. I wonder what words they had to leave out to make room for those—23 Skidoo, hepcat, groovy?

Lord, no wonder there's a generation gap. We speak different languages! With fad words always fading in and out, our hope for communication is fading fast!

But Lord, fad words aren't the ones that bother me the most.

Once upon a time, young girls were told to never cross their legs or chew gum in public because "ladies" didn't do such things. And young boys were told to always act like "gentlemen." Today shopping malls are filled with young girls and boys dressed briefly enough for the beach and their language is just as brief—it's full of words that have only four letters!

Why do these youngsters think it attractive to let something so foul and filthy spew from their mouths? Where did we go wrong, Lord? What can we do to teach them better?

Maybe there would be fewer acts of violence if the language was less violent. But we adults must teach that— by word AND example. Help us, Lord, to once again teach—and show—that there is beauty in such words as respect, consideration, gentleness, thoughtfulness—and yes, prayer and sacrifice.

~58~ Could more window seats change the world?

Way back when I was a child, Lord, I was always reading books about someone who sat in a window seat and looked out at the world. Or sat in a window seat and cozily read a book. Or sat in a window seat and daydreamed about what was to come. I always longed for a window seat of my own.

Do you guess that could be an answer for today's problems, Lord? Suppose each child had a private, cozy, snug window seat where he or she could feel safe and secure—to sit and daydream about someday, to imagine and hope, to think up ideas not limited by the small square of a TV set's eye. A child could hunker back in the corner and look at picture books or hum a song or maybe even say a prayer—without anyone criticizing this waste of time or the need to get to the next place on schedule, without anyone threatening or abusing or damaging.

We live in a dangerous world, Lord. Many children are frightened or troubled or alone or confused. They need the safety and security of a window seat of their own. Help us, Lord, to help them find it.

Long ago, you gave us a simple rule to live by and if we adults would just remember to love, we could make this world the happy, safe, secure home our children deserve. But we forget, Lord. We forget.

Forgive me, Lord. Forgive us all. And give our world and our children another chance.

~59~ The day's routine has begun—but my motor hasn't!

It's all your fault, Lord. You got my day off to a bad start. Usually when I ask your help with such a small problem— please, please, please, pretty please—you come through. Where were you this morning, Lord?

Why did you let my car decide to take a day off and just sit there, motionless, while I begged, bargained, and prayed? Did you decide to take the day off too, Lord? Didn't you see how desperate I was? Would it have been too much for you to turn over that old car's motor and charge its battery?

Did you think it was funny to watch my car smirking at me with a smile on its grill when I slammed the doors, kicked the tires, and did serious damage to my big toe?

Yes, I know it's an old, tired car, Lord, but I'm tired too. I'd like to buy a bright, shiny new car but I'd also like to take a trip to Hawaii, win the lottery, and lose twenty pounds. You and I both know, Lord, that none of the above is likely to happen.

Well, I guess you noticed I finally gave up on the car and begged a ride so I could start on my appointed rounds. But you know what happens to a day that starts like that! Now it's not just my car having trouble with its motor. I'm stalled. I'm on the side of the road while the day's routine passes me by. How am I gonna catch up?

Call out your tow truck, Lord! Take off my parking brake. Switch me out of neutral. I've got places to go and things to do. Give me a push, Lord, so I can pop my clutch and switch into high gear. Then you and I, Lord, can teach these kids a lesson about how to go at high speed and still keep the rules of the road!

~60~ Are we there yet?

Parents on vacation and teachers on field trips have four words emblazoned on their brains, never to be forgotten: "Are we there yet?" You leave in high spirits on the way to a happy time but within a few miles or a few minutes, the refrain begins: "Are we there yet?"

Next, of course, comes the chorus of other road talk: "How much longer until we get there? I'm thirsty. I'm hungry. I forgot something. I have to go to the bathroom. I think I'm going to throw up."

Well, Lord, today I want to say ALL those things. I'm thirsty and hungry—but I have things to do and places to go before I can stop for a snack. I forgot something all right—I forgot to stay in bed and skip today. I want to go the bathroom and/or throw up but there's no time to even think about that.

How much longer until I "get there," Lord? I've been doing my best to teach and guide and help and love and understand for oh-so-long now. Some days it seems like I'm almost there—I see glimmers of hope and light bulbs of understanding, I hear thank yous and hoorays, I see progress. But then something happens to remind me I'm not there yet. It was just a rest stop.

Lord, help me to not give up or give in. Help me to keep trying, keep plugging, keep bouncing along on the journey—counting cows in the fields, looking for license plates from different states, singing endless rounds of songs, and forever smiling and encouraging.

But, Lord, don't be surprised if I too ask you again tomorrow, "Are we there yet?"

~61~ Down the poor-me primrose path

Why me, Lord? Why always me? Did you paint some kind of bull's eye on my back that is visible only to the eye of the oppressor? Couldn't the world pick on somebody else for a change? Couldn't their barbs, darts, insults, and disappointments become attracted to some magnet besides ME?

Sure, I know. We all have problems. So why are mine bigger than anybody else's? Why are mine unsolvable, insurmountable, unchanging, and NOT funny any more?

What's that you say? I have a victim complex? I whine

too much? I imagine people are picking on me? I look for trouble? I worry too much? I dwell on the negative and overlook the positive? So what? Maybe I wouldn't do any of that if I didn't have all these terrible problems!

You say others have more serious things to worry about than I do? Well, that's THEIR problem. You just don't understand how serious my pain is.

You say my crown of concern is not as painful as your crown of thorns was? Oh.

I'm sorry, Lord. Deep down I know. I know my problems look so big because I magnify them. I take them out and examine them and count them and list them so I can see how Poor Me I really am!

Help, Lord. Teach me to magnify and examine and list and count my JOYS instead. Help me to look out instead of in, up instead of down. But while I'm learning, Lord, could you please do something about erasing that bull's eye?

~62~ When all else fails, get down on your biscuits and cheese

This morning, I stood my Aunt Ella in the corner, put some April Showers on my desk, and told the God Forbids we would be having Army and Navy on mashed potatoes for lunch.

Yes, Lord, I've been reading about Cockney slang, that strange and delightful language that replaces some words with other words that rhyme. I discovered that an Aunt Ella is an umbrella, April Showers are flowers, God Forbids are the words for kids and Army and Navy means gravy. Whew! Talk about English being a foreign language!

Well, Lord, maybe I've found a new way to communicate with children! Kids love that kind of game. At least, I guess they do since they are always springing new words on ME—words they've heard on TV or in the neighborhood or who knows where. Now I can spring something new on them.

I'll tell them, "You should always Bob Squash your Boat Race before you Bo-Peep." That sounds more interesting than "You should wash your face before you go to sleep." Then I'll caution them, "Never become a Tea Leaf or you could end up in the Bread and Butter." And if they get interested, I'll explain that means you should never become a thief or you could end up in the gutter.

Oh, I believe—or Adam and Eve—this is going to be an exciting new learning experience. But if it doesn't work, Lord, I'll get down on my Biscuits and Cheese and pray for you to give me another bright idea tomorrow!

~63~ Nobody tells me what to do!

Isn't it wonderful, Lord, that today we are all so free? We are independent, self-sufficient, self-reliant. Nobody tells me what to do. But I wish they would.

It was so much easier when my parents and teachers laid down the law, made me live by "house rules" and told me exactly how they expected me to behave. I hated it then. I complained, I rebelled, I felt persecuted. But now I know how easy it was.

Today it's hard, Lord. I know your rules and I want to live by them but the world's rules are so different and they keep changing all the time. I want to teach the children how to behave properly and lead a good life but the media keeps telling them they should do whatever they want to do as long as it makes them happy.

Well, maybe it would make ME happy to steal a million dollars and go off to Tahiti. Maybe the media would even approve of THAT—but I don't think YOU would.

So, Lord, please help me to teach the children to be independent enough to NOT believe everything they see on TV, hear on the radio, or read in magazines. Help me to show them that independence is important if used in the right way but there is also joy—and freedom—in DEPENDENCE.

It's great to have a friend you can DEPEND on. Life is easier when you have something solid you can COUNT on. Rules and laws may be aggravating but what kind of traffic would we have if there were no STOP signs? What kind of LIFE can we have without STOP signs? Lord, help me to explain this to the children AND to myself so the next time someone says, "Nobody can tell ME what to do!", we'll remember that you can, Lord, you can!

~64~ In the sixteenth century, what did they know?

I guess you've noticed, Lord, the recent explosion of information. Information is running out of our ears—and out of our computer discs and our VCRs and the mouths of babes.

I just learned that today one edition of the *New York Times* holds more information than the average sixteenth-century person could absorb in a lifetime. Just imagine. Those people in the sixteenth century must have had a lot more fun than we do—they didn't have to spend all their time absorbing knowledge!

Well, Lord, actually having knowledge exploding around us is great but, like antibiotics, it can't do much good until it gets into the bloodstream. And that's my job. I have some children to transfuse.

An old sage once said, "You can't plow a field by turning it over in your mind." So I better get busy plowing and trying to get a furrow planted in these small heads so they can start exploding with ideas (as if there weren't already enough ideas exploding in there!).

Help me with this important task, Lord. And even if we do live in a more challenging time than the sixteenth century, thanks for letting me be on earth now. I like this century—explosions and all!

~65~ Facing that fresh-faced firing line

Just look at all those fresh faces, Lord—so eager, so excited, so interested in learning ways to outsmart adults! How do I let them know I am friend, not foe? How do I teach myself to BE that friend?

Should I act the stern taskmaster, demanding they toe the line as well as color within it? Or should I be easy, breezy, and easy-to-pleasy?

You and I both know, Lord, that I've gotta walk that straight line that stays in the middle—teach but not preach, build up self-esteem without knocking down the security of discipline.

You and I also know, Lord, that's easier said than done. Help me, Lord. Strengthen my spine so I can stand straight and strict enough to teach them how to follow rules and learn that rules are a necessary part of an orderly society—in life as well as in school. Soften my heart so I will see which ones need a soft shoulder to cry on and which ones need a heavy hand to push. Tickle my brain so I will be wise enough to know how to guide them toward tomorrow so that when they leave my charge, they will be charged with enthusiasm for life and learning.

And Lord, help me to be always on the alert since you and I both know that right now, while I am praying, they are plotting!

~66~ My calendar is full, my desk is full, my waste basket is full—so why do I feel so empty?

Lord, why am I running on empty when this day is so full? My time, my life, my everyday is full-up and I am in danger of spilling over.

I know it all has to get done and I'm the one to do it but I still have this terrible craving to run away to an island or just to find a shade tree that I can sit under and collapse. Having a full calendar or a full desk does not necessarily mean you are leading a full life—just an overscheduled one. Having a full in-box does not mean you are one of the "in" crowd; just the opposite, it means you never have time to go out!

Forgive me, Lord, if today my complaint cup runneth over. I know I am fortunate to have "important" work to do. I know it would be depressing to have too much free time and no useful way to spend it. But I'd just like to have the chance to try it out one day—to recklessly "spend" the hours and minutes, tossing them wildly to the wind while I put up my feet and eat a hot fudge sundae.

There! I feel much better now that I've confessed all that, Lord. Now I must get back to the next item on my schedule. Oops! That was fifteen minutes ago and I missed it. I spent it, I wasted it. But I'm glad I splurged, Lord, so we could have this little talk.

Remind me to empty some real time soon so you and I can sit under that tree and have a much longer heart-to-heart. Only you, Lord, can move my gauge from EMPTY to FULL-filled!

~67~ Watch out, it's catching!

It's contagious. It spreads fast. Birds do it. Fish do it. Hippopotamuses do it. And kids do it lots. They yawn.

What could be more discouraging, Lord, than to be in the middle of a story-lesson you thought would be the most fascinating thing the children had ever heard—and see one of the kids yawn! It not only destroys your confidence, your self-image as a storyteller, your enthusiasm—it makes YOU want to yawn too!

Why is that, Lord? Why did you build in a yawn reflex? You are the ONLY one who knows for sure because I just read a report about some scientist who had conducted yawn experiments. He said yawning is one of the most common behaviors in the animal kingdom—but nobody knows the reason why.

At first it was thought that yawning indicated a lack of oxygen, but in experiments, even the people who breathed pure oxygen still yawned as much as ever. However, the experimenters did agree that yawning IS a way of increasing mental alertness. To put it simply, they explained, "Yawning may trigger the brain's production of stimulatory substances called neuro-transmitters." Yawn.

Oh well, Lord, I guess you had your reasons for giving us the yawn. It sure gets the attention of anyone dealing with children. Adults at least TRY to stifle yawns but kids don't bother. They just let it all hang out so you never have to wonder if you're being BORing.

I'd like to discuss this further, Lord, but just talking about it has made me so drowsy, I just have to—yawn—take a nap.

~68~ How can you paint rainbows with broken crayons?

Did you put something into the genes of children, Lord, that makes them feel it is absolutely necessary to tear those nice little covers off of crayons? And then break the crayons into little pieces? It seems a crime to start out with a fresh clean box of rainbow colors and end up with broken bits and smithers of waxy stubs.

And why do they never outgrow this tendency, Lord? Why do they take this with them into the higher grades and beyond? Oh, they might stop using crayons but they still break, crumble, fold, spindle, and mutilate every piece of school equipment that is issued to them.

Is this your way of giving youngsters power, Lord? Or is this your way of teaching adults that SOME things can never be taught, inculcated, or impressed on the youthful psyche?

Oh well, there ARE more important things than broken crayons. There are all those broken dreams, hopes, and hearts. And I do see a lot of them, Lord, in every group of children— even the very youngest.

Help me, Lord, to reach out to them and give them back their rainbows even when their crayons are broken. Help me to be patient with their nervous energy, to try to harness their destructiveness and turn it into usefulness, to try to heal their brokenness by showing them your bridge, your rainbow of hope.

And, Lord, please let the new budget allow me some unbroken crayons so I can donate these little red, yellow, and blue scraps to a wax museum!

~69~ Thinking can be dangerous to your tomorrows!

A wise old saying warns, "You are today what you thought yesterday." Oh, oh! What did I think yesterday? And what will tomorrow be like if it depends on what I'm thinking today?

Well, I'm thinking about a plaque that hangs on my wall. If I pay attention to what it says, it reminds me to "Feel deeply, enjoy simply, think freely, take risks, love, be who you really are."

I wish I could teach that lesson to the children—but first, I have to learn it myself! I DO feel deeply—that I should be doing all those OTHER things! It's easy for me to enjoy simply and I try to think freely, but taking risks is a toughy. And what does love mean today? People throw that word around so much now that is has lost a lot of its meaning and its glory.

And I am still trying to figure out who I really am, Lord.

I know the children are struggling with the same dilemmas. Most children feel deeply. A dog with a sore foot can make them sob. And it's so natural for them to think freely and freshly. They LOVE to take risks—all too often dangerous ones. And they are often dramatically generous with their love.

But they too are trying to figure out who they really are. And it is probably harder for children today than it was in the past. They face so many choices, so many dangers, so many temptations.

Help me, Lord, to never stifle their joy and openness. Help me to encourage their originality and the way they see things with the newness of youth. Help me to teach them to make wise choices and think good thoughts today so they will grow toward good tomorrows.

~70~ Out with the old, in with the new, can lead to boo hoo

New! I'm beginning to hate that word, Lord. New methods, new procedures, new forms to fill out, new questions to answer, new challenges to meet, new focus, new hocus-pocus. How can I make everything NEW when the only tool I've got to work with is the same OLD me!

I have enough trouble just breaking in new shoes or trying a new haircut. One reason I've been driving the same old car for so long is that I can't stand the thought of a car dealer urging me to buy a new one!

Lord, you should understand my problem. Every year, every season, every day, every second, you are working on new creations. You turn winter's stark trees into leafy green feathery shade. You turn bare branches into blossoming beauties. You join tiny cells to form rosy-cheeked babies. And you keep making a fresh new sunrise every single morning. So why am I complaining to you? Next to yours, my job should be a snap!

But Lord, I am not all-powerful, all-knowing, all-loving like you. I am just me. Just plain little ordinary me. And I am tired. Help me, Lord.

Help me grow and change like your universe. Help me see and appreciate the newness in your creation so that I can reflect it to the children.

~71~ Now let's not have any more of that!

Lord, a famous comedian once told about the time when he was in the fifth grade and answered the teacher with a little joke. The whole class roared and even the teacher couldn't hold back a small smile. But then she said, "Now, let's not have any more of that."

That happens so many times, Lord—in a class or a Scout meeting or anywhere children are gathered together. A child does or says something that is clever or funny or different and the adult in charge immediately says, "Now let's not have any more of that." We HAVE to do that,

Lord. We HAVE to choke back the giggle or the slightest bit of approval so we can keep order and carry on.

But, Lord, that same comedian added that the day he got the class to laugh AND the teacher to smile ever so slightly, he KNEW what he wanted to do and be when he grew up. He had his goal and he worked to achieve it. I have also read about writers or artists or doctors or whatevers who told of how a small incident in childhood sent them in the direction that became their livelihoods, their lives.

Lord, there is such a fine line between keeping order and squelching or discouraging a child with a talent or a dream. Nudge me, Lord, when I begin to cross over that line. Help me to know whether the proper response is a small smile or a big frown.

Fill my head with wisdom and my heart with under-standing so I can use just the right inflection when I say, "Now let's not have any more of that!"

~72~ I'm not a mind reader so how can I be a mind molder?

Sometimes, Lord, I think it would be EASIER to be a mind reader than to be a mind molder! Here I am with all these fresh young minds, with the opportunity to mold them and turn them into responsible, thinking people and it's a great opportunity—but I think I'd rather be making a Jello mold!

Jello may wiggle, but not as much as children. Jello may refuse to "set" some of the time but children refuse that MOST of the time. And Jello molds usually look so bright and shiny and shaped perfectly when you finish working with them. Children often look half-asleep, a bit grimy, and ALL out of shape when you finish with THEM.

Whenever I stir shredded carrots or fruit salad into Jello, I know what the result will be. Whenever I try to stir up new ideas into wiggly kids I never know what to expect. I say one thing and they hear another. I explain and they question. I "prove" and they doubt. I try and they often don't!

Well, Lord, maybe it's a good idea I'm NOT a mind reader. It's probably best that I NOT know what they're really thinking! So thank you, Lord, for making me a mind molder instead. Help me to always be careful to teach the truth instead of half-truths. Help me to do MY homework so I will understand what I am talking about before I start talking.

And, Lord, thank you for not letting the children be mind readers either. It's best THEY not know what thoughts smolder in this molder!

~73~ Time flies but can you catch more of it with honey than vinegar?

It's a vinegary day, Lord. I do not feel like letting honey droppeth from my tongue. My time is flying because "other people" keep dropping by to use up my minutes and open the window so my hours fly right out.

I know I should be able to find a honeyed way to tell them to get lost but the vinegar keeps rising up in my throat. The only reason it hasn't spewed forth is because it couldn't get past my gritted teeth.

Do you know how I feel, Lord? When you were on earth, people were always following you around too, wanting you to speak to them, come to their house, or just let them touch your garment. As I remember, you also got a little "pushed" sometimes—and that's when you went off to a desert or a mountaintop to be alone. Well, I guess that's what I should do too.

I should MAKE some free time and find a spot to be alone for a little while—with no one around except YOU. And for once, instead of doing all the talking, I should listen so you can talk to ME and gently soothe me and fill my tongue with honey again.

That's what I'll do, Lord—SOON. But for right now, Lord, could you please send those "other people" on a detour so I can get some work done and make it through this vinegary day! Thanks, Lord—you're a honey!

~74~ I wonder as I wander and I wander as I wonder

I wonder why my checkbook never balances the first time. I wonder why I never learned to ice skate. I wonder why that plant on the window sill looked so beautiful for two days and then died overnight. I wonder why my mind wanders so much.

Yes, Lord, I've been wandering among the wonders today. It was fun but not as much fun as wandering among YOUR wonders. How did you ever dream up such things as icebergs and hot lava, waterfalls and water buffaloes, honeysuckle and honey bees, pelicans and awkward and awesome people? They're all very interesting— some more so than others, but all wonder-filled.

Help me, Lord, to show the children how to look for and notice all the big and little wonders you've planted in the world for us to discover.

Rachel Carson said, "If a child is to keep alive his inborn sense of wonder, he needs the companionship of at least one adult who can share it, rediscovering with him the joy, excitement, and mystery of the world we live in."

Help me to be that adult for any child who is without such a companion. Help me to lead—and to follow.

~75~ Just because

Why does everyone think I have to have a reason for everything, Lord? Why has our society started analyzing and examining our every word and every action? I am not a specimen to be studied under a microscope—I am simply a child of God and a fun person (once you get to know me). Isn't that enough?

I don't know WHY I like bright colors better than pale ones or WHY I like sitting on the front porch in a rocker during a rainstorm or WHY I hate ketchup on a hamburger or, for that matter, why I say ketchup instead of catsup. And I don't care. If somebody wants an answer, here it is: JUST BECAUSE.

Of course, I am not happy when a kid gives ME an answer like that. I want a reason the homework was not done, the waste basket not emptied, the chore not completed. I think it's reasonable to expect reasons for such things. But I don't think it necessary to badger a kid about every little like or dislike, every strange haircut or bitten fingernail, every word or action. Sometimes children too have a good reason to answer, JUST BECAUSE.

Lord, I know children need—and deserve—SOME privacy, some way to express their individuality. Please keep me on the lookout for danger signals so I will know when it is prudent to intrude. But also remind me that some things are just none of my business!

And, Lord, the next time someone becomes imprudent and intrudes by asking me the "reason" I don't like to be analyzed, please send a lightning bolt in their direction—just because.

~76~ If canines are cunning teachers, what can I learn from them?

Robert Benchley said, "A dog teaches a boy fidelity, perseverance, and to turn around three times before lying down."

If Benchley was right, every boy AND every girl should get a dog immediately. I've been trying to teach fidelity and perseverance and so far, all I've noticed them doing is turning around three times before they lie down, sit down, or get on the school bus.

But children HAVE taught ME that I must have fidelity and perseverance. Without those two guiding lights, I'd never find my way through the tunnel each day.

Well, to be honest, most children DO have fidelity. Once you get them on your side, they become faithful followers and devoted friends. And they DO have perseverance, especially when they want something or want to DO something! They will ask you over and over again, until their perseverance wears down yours OR your perseverance finally convinces them that the answer is NO.

Thank you, Lord, for dogs and boys and girls and fidelity and perseverance. The world would be a terrible place without any of those. And help me, Lord, to live and teach in a way that will earn the fidelity of the children and inspire them to have fidelity to friends, family, goals, and virtue. And please persevere in YOUR patience with us, Lord, even if we DO all seem to have that habit of turning around three times before we can fetch, sit, stay—or get some work done!

~77~ Daisies and dandelions can make chains that bind!

No wonder we call children dandy-lions, Lord. They look so bright and dandy and they have the courage of lions. And children love dandelions, Lord. They pick them and present a grimy handful to you as though they are giving you a bouquet of rare orchids. We can heartlessly pull dandelions up, stomp on them, and spray them with poison—but within a few days, there they are again, sprouting their cheery yellow smiles all over the lawn.

The daisies are just as hardy. They aren't considered weeds but they DO come up sturdily every year and bloom and bloom with very little care or attention. And the children love them too. They pick them and make daisy chains to decorate the dog or to hang proudly around a friend's neck.

Why is it, Lord, that these same children who are so happy with so little will grow in a few years to demand so much?

The chains of memory will bind adults forever to those simpler years but the children will be drawn into forgetfulness by the lure of ads for more and more expensive goodies.

Help us all, Lord, to remember that the simple things are still fun and worthwhile. Help us to show this to our children. And help them to shake off the chains of giveme, I-want, I've-gotta-have, and return to the happier and simpler joys of childhood—chains of daisies and dandelions.

~78~ When did discipline become a dirty word?

Why am I always at the wrong place at the wrong time, Lord? When I was growing up, children were to be seen but not heard. Discipline was IN. Adults ruled, children obeyed. Now I finally get to be an adult and discipline is OUT. Adults no longer rule, children seldom obey. How did you let this happen, Lord?

It's my turn and I want to be obeyed. I want discipline to become an admired word again instead of a dirty one. Well, I don't mean MEAN discipline. I mean constructive discipline.

It seems that discipline comes from the same root word as disciple—and that shows how we should all act. Help me, Lord, help us ALL to be disciples, showing children the value of being your followers, of obeying your rules, of leading a disciplined life so it can be a good, moral, ethical life.

There are enough dirty words being tossed about today, Lord. Help us to find again the merit and the potential of the words discipline and disciple.

And, Lord, I know I am not really at the wrong place at the wrong time. This is MY time, the time you gave me—so it is the right time. Help me to make the most of it.

~79~ Caught in the middle—again!

All of my friends are having a mid-life crisis, Lord. Some of them aren't old enough to be considered middle and the rest of us are pretending we're not—but the crisis is real. Since we are all constantly being pulled at both ends by scheduled necessities and unscheduled emergencies, the middle was bound to show up way off schedule.

We keep meeting, discussing, and considering what we can do about it. We think we should explore new horizons, discover new dimensions, opt for new outlets—in other words, earn a little extra money to put new elastic into our overstretched budgets.

We thought we might sell gravy door-to-door and call it "Mother's Smother" or sandwiches known as "Mamma's Salami" or astrological forecasts from Mommy the Swami. We considered decorated ladders marketed as "Teacher's Reacher," drawings titled "Principal's Prints," or food products like "Teach's Peaches" or "Counselor's Consommé." Yes, I know, Lord, we're reaching. But that's what you have to do when you're caught in the middle!

You know, Lord, we won't do any of those things but they're fun to talk about anyhow. The grass always looks greener on the highways and byways but we'll stick with the crabgrass on the playground and go on crabbing about our mildewed middle.

What else can we do, Lord? With all those scheduled and unscheduled commitments, we don't have TIME to conquer the world just yet! But there's always tomorrow, tomorrow ...

~80~ I think, therefore I am; I tire, therefore I feint

I'm so tired, Lord, I feel like fainting but I can't so I feint. I think, therefore I know I can't answer all questions or all needs. When I get full up to the overflow, that's when I feint.

Sometimes I know one child needs more of my time—but there IS no more time—so I dodge, I parry, I postpone. I say, "Let's talk tomorrow ... let's each think about that and get back together next week." I hold out hope instead of help and pray the bandage will stick until I can get back to the wound.

Lord, I want to do more but I am so tired. I have answered so many questions and tried to fill so many needs and once in a while, I have to admit that I have needs of my own. I HAVE to feint and take a little time for myself or I really will faint.

Teach me, Lord, how to feint properly so neither the children nor I will become faint-of-heart.

~81~ Do I have to give these kids the coat off my back?

The storm is brewing, Lord. I can feel it coming. They're starting to mumble, grumble, and cast furtive glances at me. These kids are getting ready to blow.

I've tried everything else to calm the storm. I guess I'm gonna have to give them the coat off my back!

You see, Lord, I once read that's what camel drivers do. It seems that camels just naturally have bad attitudes. A camel can act calm for a while, but it resents its driver and the resentment grows and grows until one day, the camel suddenly goes berserk!

But a good camel driver can sense when trouble is coming. And when he thinks his camel is ready to rebel, he takes off his coat and gives it to the camel! The camel bites it, stomps on it, shakes it, and tears the coat to pieces. Once the camel thinks the driver has been punished enough, the camel calms down. Then the driver and the camel go on about their business.

I wonder if camel drivers can report coat-loss on their income tax. Probably not. I wonder if I could report it. Probably not. So I guess I better find a better way to ensure peace and calm. Maybe I'll read a nice gentle story to soothe them. Nah. Maybe we could take a nature walk. Nah. They'd probably run away—or I would.

Maybe I just better get on with the day and stop mumbling, grumbling, and casting furtive glances at them!

~82~ All show-n-tells are not equal

Today, Lord, I heard about a man who gave a nature talk to a second-grade class. He showed them a video of a volcano with molten lava pouring out and running toward the sea. When the lava hit the ocean, steam spewed high, a mile into the air. The children watched wide-eyed. Afterward, the man passed around a chunk of lava for each child to feel and hold.

One little girl gingerly touched the lava and then cupped her hands around it. She looked up at the man in awe and said in a hushed voice, "It's still warm."

Isn't that wonderful, Lord? She was so engrossed with the idea of that molten lava, she could imagine warmth. I wish I could reach the children I teach in that same way, Lord.

When I speak to them, help me to give them awe instead of yawn. Teach me how to really talk WITH, not only TO, children. Help me to not just fill their heads with knowledge but to also stir their imagination and fill them with excitement, joy, and an appreciation of all the wonders of your world.

Give me the ability, Lord, to show, to tell—and to inspire.

~83~ It's hard to teach kids to walk and talk, but why is it so much harder to teach them to sit down and be quiet?

Children are so adorable, Lord, when they take that first step and say that first word. Why aren't they as adorable when they keep jumping up and down out of their seat? Why aren't they as adorable when they're always talking when they should be listening?

I know to be able to walk and talk are great blessings. I thank you for those, Lord. But I ask you to help me to be gentle yet firm so that I can also teach children the value of sitting down and being quiet.

Maybe we adults are the ones who have taught young ones to NOT listen since we are so often guilty of not listening to THEM. Help me to listen more carefully, Lord. Remind me of how much today's children NEED a listening ear and help me set a good example. There are so many basics that NEED to be learned NOW so the children will have a foundation to build on for their future. But who can learn a lesson that is not heard?

So Lord, please show me how to command and demand attention and respect. Help me convince those children it's important to look AND listen before you leap!

~84~ It must be true—it's in the book!

The famous writer, Dorothy Parker, once reviewed a book by saying, "It is not a book to be tossed aside lightly. It should be thrown with great force."

I know just what she meant, Lord. I keep finding books that fit right into that category. The terrifying thing is that some of those books are written by "experts" on child guidance, motivation, ethics, goal-setting, and whatever. I often wonder who taught these people who are trying to teach us how to teach children.

One problem is that some of those authors base all their "teachings" on worldly values, not on YOUR values, Lord. So please, Lord, help me to be choosy. Guard my gullibility. Hold my hand and show me which books I should cherish as treasures and which I should pitch or even throw with great force!

You know how much I love books, Lord. Whenever I'm missing in action, I can be found with my nose in a book. Whenever there's a minute to spare, I spend it poring over a page. Teach me, Lord, to be selective in what I read—and what I believe.

Of course, Lord, I know YOU inspired a book that is filled with truthful teachings and gentle guidance. But to be honest, Lord, I can't always understand YOUR book. Sometimes your message gets through to me but other days I need a little lighter reading.

On those days, Lord, remind me of the words of another famous person, Sir Francis Bacon. He said, "Some books are to be tasted, others to be swallowed, and some few to be chewed and digested." Teach me, Lord, to not bite off more than I should chew!

~85~ If all the news is bad, why do I need to hear it?

Just once, Lord, I'd like the six o'clock news to tell me something worth remembering. I'm tired of hearing stuff I would like to forget.

If we believe all the "news," it would be easy to conclude that we have good reasons to live in bitterness, hatred, hostility. But who would really want to live like that?

What makes it even sadder is the fact that our children are listening to those broadcasts too. We used to wish the younger generation would be more interested in the world around them instead of being so focused on themselves. Now we still want that, but we don't want them ONLY exposed to the BAD side, the under side, the bitter side of the world!

Help us, Lord, to recognize the beauty along with the pain. Some of the children have already learned that lesson for themselves. I read about a young boy who was dying of cancer. He sat down and made a list of all the good things he and his family had done together, all the fun times, the happy memories. Before he died, he gave this list to his parents and told them he wanted them to make a special effort to remember the good days—not just the sad, painful hospital days.

Please help us to teach all children to be like that boy, Lord, and dwell on the good news of the earth instead of being influenced by or becoming a part of the bad news.

Help us to give them a sense of joy, of being alive—a sense of being an important and good part of your world. They say misery loves company. Help us, Lord, to refuse the invitation.

~86~ How can I find a weigh out before the weigh in?

Lord, I just learned that human bones are 50 percent water, that humans shed one and a half million hairs in a lifetime and lose 105 pounds of skin by the age of seventy. Now it's really not great news that I have watery bones and am leaving a trail of hairs instead of bread crumbs as I travel the road of life. But that bit about 105 pounds got my attention.

Lord, instead of losing a little each day for seventy years, could I take an advance and just lose ten pounds by next week's school reunion? I promise to pay it back by the time I'm seventy. In fact, I could probably pay it back by week after next!

Yes, Lord, I know today's society has become obsessed with weight and I am a product of today's society. I know that I should be thinking of matters more weighty than the fact that my bathroom scale squeaks and complains every time I step on it. I know that the only way to weigh less is to lead a more disciplined life. I know that I have been trying to teach the children to lead a more disciplined life and here I am complaining because I have not learned my own lesson.

I'm sorry, Lord. I promise to do better. But, Lord, if I can't lose ten pounds by next week, could you at least help me find an outfit to wear that will make me LOOK thinner—and richer and smarter and current and successful and—oh. I'm sorry, Lord. Never mind.

~87~ Gimme, gimme, gimme

I want it ALL. Buy one, get one free. Charge now, pay when they catch you. Grab all you can get while nobody's looking. Get your fair share—you have a right to it.

When did those become the new commandments, Lord? I don't remember your mentioning them. I remember something about being your brother's keeper, learning from the lilies of the field, and coveting NOT.

When did children decide the world owed them the good life? When did they start expecting everything for nothing? When did they start demanding a free ride and a free lifestyle? Why do they think they should get it ALL—not as a reward for good behavior or good marks, not as a result of hard work, but as a RIGHT?

We both know when and why, Lord. They expect and

demand because they have been taught this by the media, world leaders, role models, and the adults they see in their everyday life. Thankfully, ALL kids do not expect ALL. Some are still being taught about your love and commandments, about integrity and honor, about the value of hard work and high morals. Help us, Lord, to change that "some" to "most."

Help us have the courage, Lord, to speak up and speak out, to demand greater integrity from our leaders—and from ourselves. The future is in the hands of our children but those children are in OUR hands now. Help us to give them a strong "hand up" to tomorrow by teaching them YOUR way of life, not the world's.

~88~ Have I been speaking in shorthand?

Yep, nope, notnow, inaminute, pulleeze. Lord, have I been wondering why those children keep giving me shorthand answers— without realizing I am the one who taught them the trick?

Am I always in such a hurry scurry, that I give them only grunts and nods when they ask questions or sidle up to me wanting to talk about nothing—or maybe something? Do I respond with warmed-over fast-talk when they are yearning for a wholesome, home-made, sit-down conversation?

Am I the one who taught them to ignore me as I do them, to be too busy to explore any subject beyond a noncommittal yes, no, maybe? Have I been complaining about their lack of attention and slovenly responses when they have only been following the leader?

Oh, Lord, help me to do better. Remind me that if I give these children only shorthand, short shrift, shortcuts, and short circuits, it could have long-range effects—all bad.

Help me, Lord, to stop short and listen long.

~89~ A gaggle of geese, a covey of doves, a clamor of children

---

Lord, if there were a category name to describe a group of children—as there are names for animal groupings—it would have to be *clamor*. Or possibly *chaos, crisis,* or *circumvention.*

Wherever children are gathered together, you have a clamor. This often leads to some crisis, then chaos—and when you try to untangle it all, the kids will do everything to circumvent your efforts.

Well, why not! A child's job description includes the responsibility to drive adults bananas and cause confusion wherever and whenever possible. And they do their jobs well.

If only they would do some of their other jobs as well! And if only they would leave behind the clamor and confusion when they leave childhood instead of carrying it with them—to teendom and even beyond! But, Lord, perhaps I ask too much, expect too much.

And yet if I don't ask, don't tell, don't challenge, how can these children ever realize what will be expected of them in the adult world? Today there's an awful lot of together-ness, Lord, and that can make the clamor almost unbearable. But there's also a lot of separated-ness and that can be even more unbearable.

Help us to find and teach the happy medium, Lord—some clamor, some quiet, some sharing, some working alone. But, Lord, for just the next ten minutes, could you please inspire them to be quiet? This clamor is giving me clamorphobia.

~90~ Why is my survival kit held together with paper clips?

Only a teacher or a parent could think of 369 ways to use a paper clip. But we HAVE to think like that, Lord. Improvisation is the key to survival!

Most people would look at a bobby pin, safety pin, or paper clip and think it could only be used for the purpose the inventor visualized. Not us. We visualize using such utensils to get cracker crumbs out of the tracks of sliding doors, to gouge out crayon bits stuck in zippers, to remove hardened peanut butter that is cemented to desks, tables, chairs, and small people, to ... well, you get the picture, Lord.

Help us, Lord, to be just as creative and inventive in removing sticky ideas that children have gotten from the television and allowed to harden in their brains. Help us to unglue the wise-guy stuff and replace it with some real wisdom.

But speaking of hardened brains, Lord, today mine has gotten stuck in the no-go position. Have you got a paper clip handy?

~91~ This constant need to share, bare, and care is wearing me down— and out!

I DO care, Lord, but I'm tired of always talking about it. I'm tired of baring my soul in groups of people I don't even know. I don't mind sharing with my family but I'm tired of telling all to people with whom I wouldn't even want to share a pizza!

Some businesses even expect executives to have sharing sessions where they sit around and tell stories about their deepest problems. A man explains why the wart on his Great Aunt Sue's chin made him grow up with the fear of doing chin-ups. A woman tells why she can never ride in a red car because her father refused to let her eat an ice cream cone in his new red car when she was six years old.

One woman told me she solved the problem of sharing. She "confesses" a made-up story of her wonderful childhood and reveals that in both high school and college, she was prom queen, valedictorian, and a cheerleader—and she supposes that's why she is always so successful today. It's just her destiny!

Well, Lord, I know that some people DO have serious problems that stem from childhood or adolescence and it does help to talk about some things—but not EVERYthing with EVERYone. Only you, Lord, can understand and heal some of our problems. Maybe if we could teach the children to spend as much time in prayer as they do in "share," they would grow up healthier and happier.

Help us to do that, Lord. Help ME to do that. Help me to share my worn-down-and-outness with you so you can share your healing, welcoming care with me.

~92~ Is my face red—or blue?

I should be blushing today, Lord. I made another boo-boo. I should admit I'm wrong, hang my head, grovel, and apologize. My face should be red.

But it isn't yet, Lord. It's yellow. I don't want to admit I made a mistake. I don't want to be embarrassed. I want to take the coward's way out and pretend it never happened and hope nobody will notice.

All this time, I've taught the children to never ever tell a lie, to always admit when you're wrong, to take your medicine like a good boy or girl, to be brave and true no matter how much it hurts. I want to forget my own lesson. I don't want it to hurt, Lord. I just want it to go away.

But I know it won't. Even if nobody notices and nobody ever finds out what I did, I know. And you know.

Wipe that yellow off my face, Lord. I know it was my fault and I have to face up to my error.

But, Lord, please help me to be more careful and more conscientious and more alert so I will never ever again make such a stupid mistake, the kind of mistake that can turn me red in the face—and green around the gills and white around the mouth and blue in the soul.

I love all your colors, Lord, but this kind of a rainbow I can do without!

~93~ My room runneth over

Where did it all come from, Lord? All those books, doodads, stubby pencils, and used-up ballpoints? Where did I get so many Magic Markers that have lost their magic, so many projects that never got finished, so many "ideas to file" that never got filed?

My room runneth over, Lord—and it is just a reflection of my brain. Some people have junk drawers. I have a junk room and a brain to match. My brain is stuffed with things I will never need to remember, things I would like to forget, trivia I will never be asked (since I've given up the hope of making my fortune on a quiz show), and little-known facts nobody else wants to know.

I can repeat plots of movies I saw as a teenager but can't remember the name of my neighbor's teenager who just shouted hello across the lawn. I have carefully filed away the menu from the place that was once my favorite restaurant but don't have a clue about what to fix for dinner tonight.

When are you going to help me clean house, Lord? When are you going to help me pitch out the trash so there will be room for some treasure? How can I pass on golden bits of wisdom to the children when my mind keeps humming tunes of "golden oldies" and remembering the time I left my heart on the Golden Gate bridge? I need help, Lord, I need help.

Sort through my many files, Lord. Show me how to delete the inconsequentials and put in long-term storage only the things I need to remember—like the lessons you taught me and the love you gave me—in the hope I would pass them on to others. Thank you, Lord. My heart runneth over with gratitude.

~94~ Tying up the loose ends

Oops! There's another one. Every time I think I've tied up all those loose ends, Lord, another comes undone. Maybe it's because I have the habit of pushing things under the carpet—only to see them work their way out at the most inopportune times.

Yes, I admit it. I "save time" by sticking things in, under, or behind. And then of course I have to go back and spend more time getting them out again, doing them over again—tying up all those loose ends.

A wise person once said that we don't have enough time to do things right but we have enough time to do them OVER. That's what I've been doing, Lord—too many overs and not enough rights.

How can I teach the children to do it right the FIRST time so they won't have to do it OVER when I am guilty of putting away until later instead of now, and trying to survive in this tangled web I wove of loose ends! Again, Lord—HELP! I know that if I let myself become overcommitted, I will never have enough time for the preparation and planning necessary to get things done properly. I

KNOW I should say NO when there's too little time to add one more thing to my overcrowded days. But, Lord, there are so many projects that SOMEBODY has to do, so many fun things I WANT to do, so many challenging things I think I SHOULD do. How can I sort it all out?

Give me strength, Lord. Muscle up my will power AND my won't power. Whisper to me when to say yes, no, or maybe. And help me to turn all my loose ends into happy endings!

~95~ Bumper snickers

How did we ever drive down the road of life, Lord, before someone decided to make clever bumper stickers? Maybe we drove more carefully when we weren't forever reading bumpers, but we sure didn't have as much fun.

I like the sticker that says, "I know about STRESSED. It's desserts spelled backwards." Then there's this wise one: "There's nothing wrong with teenagers that reasoning with them won't aggravate." And the one that hits especially close to home admits, "Time flies when you don't know what you're doing."

But today, Lord, I spotted the best yet. It simply said, "If you can read this, thank a teacher."

Isn't that wonderful, Lord? Adults often tell stories about a favorite teacher who "changed my direction in life," "made me realize learning could be fun," "got me excited about reading books," etc. And sometimes those adults go back and seek out that teacher to say thanks.

Lots of children are also thankful for the opportunity to learn. They show their thanks in many ways. That's why teachers are often "paid" in an exchange other than dollars. That's why teachers AND parents still believe that though their jobs may be hard and their hours long, the fringe benefits make it all worthwhile.

So speaking of thanks, Lord, thank YOU for children—who give us hugs and hope and keep us on our toes. As another bumper sticker says, "The greatest aid to adult education is children!"

~96~ If my job is so important, why ain't I rich?

Yes, I said "ain't," Lord. The new dictionary now lists *ain't* as an official word. All these years, we've been trying to teach children to never say ain't and now the dictionary says, "never mind."

Oh well, there are many more important things we've been trying to teach children too and now the world says, "never mind."

But I'm off the subject again, Lord. Why is it that basketball players, weather forecasters, and garbage collectors who belong to a good union ALL make more money than I do? If my job is so important, why ain't I rich?

What's that you say, Lord? The apostles weren't rich either? Oh! And they had a VERY important job. And Mother Teresa never had much money, in spite of her important work. O.K., Lord, I guess money ain't everything.

I see now that my job is important and rich in potential. Helping little empty heads grow into mature thinking people is not an easy job but it IS mine. And I am grateful for it. I know that I have the power to influence the children in my life for good or for better. I know that I may be their only bridge between ignorance and knowledge, between a moral life and wantonness, between a sad existence and a joyful, productive one. Wow! What power!

I DO have an important job. Oh, Lord, ain't it grand!

~97~ Can lists make you listless?

Lord, I heard about a lady who made a list of all the things she asked you for in her prayers. Later, she would check the list and she was always surprised to find how many requests had been answered—but usually NOT in the way she had expected!

Lord, I make lists all day, every day—things to remember, chores to be done, calls to be made, things to be picked up, books to read, videos to watch. But I've never made a list of my prayer requests. And yet, I know, Lord, that if I did, I too would find that you had answered many of my prayers in your own way, not mine.

I remember the time I prayed desperately to get a new job in my favorite town but instead got a new job in a different town—and it changed my life forever and for better. I remember the time I prayed for the owners to accept our bid on a house we wanted to buy but someone else bid higher and we lost. Then, just a few weeks later, we were able to buy a house we liked even better. There have been so many times, Lord, when you have saved me from myself.

Help me, Lord, to explain this strange prayer process to children. Help me to gently remind them that you always answer prayers, but sometimes the answer is no and sometimes the answer is a different (and often better) one than what they had imagined.

Too many lists can make me listless, Lord, so I'm not going to start listing my prayer requests. But then again I don't NEED a list to remember your surprising and loving answers.

~98~ I'm sorry, I cannot give you that information

Why do cats purr and parrots talk? Why don't spiders get caught in their own webs? Why does my skin get all wrinkly when I take a bath? And why don't I laugh when I bump my funny bone?

Ah yes, kids never run out of these kinds of questions. And when they ask, "Why does hair turn white?" I tell them, "It's because you asked so many questions, my head cracked and all the color ran out!"

They giggle and say, "But YOUR hair's not white." And I say, with great surprise, "It isn't? I thought sure I felt all the color running out about ten questions ago."

Oh, Lord, it CAN be fun to talk to kids! They probably don't think it's as much fun to talk to me because I'm so corny, but I love hearing a giggle and seeing one of those wide-eyed double-takes on the small face of an often so innocent child.

Thank you, Lord, for letting me associate with the "in" group—the group that's often in line at the water fountain, in momentary disgrace, in over their heads, in a muddle or a mud puddle. And I don't mean just the little kids, Lord. That description can fit a kid of any age—even my age.

Yes, Lord, I am with them and for them and just like them. And I LIKE them. Please help me to stay "in like" with them even when they ask questions I can't answer. Help me to inspire as well as instruct, no matter how incomprehensible, infernal, infuriating, or innumerable their questions may be. It's the only way we can all stay "in" sane!

~99~ You can't judge a book by its cover, even if it is hand-drawn

Look at all those messy book covers, Lord. They were so fresh and new just a few weeks ago. And now they're a mess. Most of them started out nice, neat, and generic, but soon the kids began to doodle. Now those books are covered with the strangest looking designs and scribbles—and, I have to admit, a few really eye-catching drawings too!

Who would suspect that under all that graffiti are pages of fascinating facts, hair-raising tales of historic adventures, news of scientific experiments and discoveries, and inspiring stories of heroes and heroines. I guess that's what they mean when they say, "You can't judge a book by its cover!"

Help me remember that same lesson when I look at the children, Lord. Some of them are more attractive than others; some are smarter or funnier or lazier or poorer or just plain needier. Some need more love; some need more understanding; some need a good dose of "Pay attention! Now!" But they are each unique and loveable because they were made by you. Help me see that and act on that, Lord.

Help me see around and through—so that I will never judge a child by his or her cover.

~100~ How growing pains can turn adults into blooming idiots

The person who invented time-lapse photography must have been a teacher or a parent. It's mind-boggling to watch a video that shows how a tiny flower, ever so slowly, yet ever so swiftly, opens into a full-blown blossom. And that's the way it is with children, Lord.

We think a tiny baby will never grow enough to stop crying all night and then, ever so slowly, yet ever so swiftly, the baby turns into a toddler who pulls everything off shelves and runs across the floor saying things like, "Me wuv you."

It's the same with the school children. There they are in kindergarten learning how to color inside the lines or "express themselves" by smearing crayons on the toys, the table, and other kids. We think they'll never grow out of that stage. And then, ever so slowly, yet ever so swiftly, they grow as tall as we are and learn how to keep the rules or break them, talk brilliantly on some subjects that are new to us or talk unintelligibly, using words known only to their peers.

Help me, Lord, to treasure every stage, every phase, every growth spurt. Help me to know what to demand and what to allow so the children will grow, ever so slowly, yet ever so swiftly, into the loving, virtuous, worthwhile adults you created them to be.

And thank you Lord for all those ages and stages. Trying to meet their challenges and grow in wisdom as they grow in height just might keep me young!

~101~ Maybe I'm on the wrong mission impossible!

Lord, why didn't I choose a life-work that would take me to the foreign missions? Sure, I might have to learn to fight lions and mosquitoes or snow-shoe across frozen waste. But could that be more hazardous than Monday morning traffic or more chaotic than the school picnic or more scary than a pair of little eyes staring into mine and asking over and over again, "Why?"

Have I missed my calling, Lord? Did I make a mistake in choosing a Mission Impossible instead of a foreign mission?

Well, I guess not. I was never very good at camping out so a life-work that includes scorpions and spiders would probably not light up my life. And a person who gets carsick on the way to the mall probably should not choose a mission that might include donkey rides or rafting down rapids. I guess I better settle for the mission I have.

Some days it's tempting to want to run away somewhere, anywhere, but I know deep down that I am where I belong. So I will remind myself that I can do MORE than just survive—I can revive and look alive! I will remind myself that I am doing YOUR work, Lord. And I will be dutiful and work and teach and pray and set a good example. (Or at least, I'll do some of those things.) And I will also find time to sing songs and giggle and invite someone to share a pizza. THEN, Lord, my mission WON'T be impossible.

I don't have to run away to be a missionary. I already am one.